Adventures in Canadian History

THE CAPTURE OF DETROIT

Books for Younger Readers by Pierre Berton

The Golden Trail
The Secret World of Og

ADVENTURES IN CANADIAN HISTORY

The Capture of Detroit
The Death of Isaac Brock

PIERRE BERTON

The Battles of the War of · 1812 ·

THE CAPTURE OF DETROIT

ILLUSTRATIONS BY SCOTT CAMERON

M&S

An M&S Paperback Original from
McClelland & Stewart Inc.
The Canadian Publishers

An M&S Paperback Original from McClelland & Stewart Inc.

First printing April 1991

Canadian Cataloguing in Publication Data

Berton, Pierre, 1920–
  The capture of Detroit

(Adventures in Canadian history. The battles of the
War of 1812)
"An M&S paperback."
Includes index.
ISBN 0-7710-1425-2

1. Detroit (Mich.) – Surrender to the British,
1812 – Juvenile literature. 2. Canada – History –
War of 1812 – Campaigns – Juvenile literature.*
3. United States – History – War of 1812 – Campaigns –
Juvenile literature. I. Cameron, Scott (Scott R.).
II. Title. III. Series: Berton, Pierre, 1920– .
Adventures in Canadian history. The battles of the
War of 1812.

E356.D4B47 1991   j973.5'23   C91-093136-4

Series design by Tania Craan
Cover and interior illustrations by Scott Cameron
Maps by James Loates

Typesetting by Pickwick
Printed and bound in Canada

McClelland & Stewart Inc.
The Canadian Publishers
481 University Avenue
Toronto, Ontario
M5G 2E9

Contents

Maps appear on pages viii-ix and page 25

Adventures in Canadian History

The Capture of Detroit

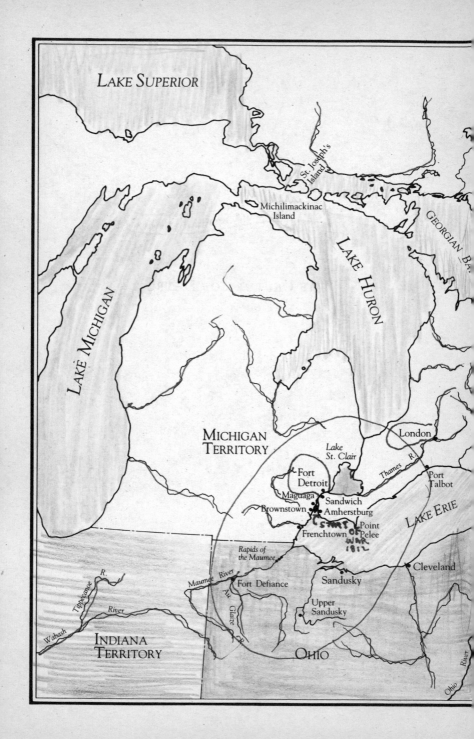

LAKE SUPERIOR

Michilimackinac
Island

St. Joseph's
Island

LAKE HURON

GEORGIAN BA.

LAKE MICHIGAN

MICHIGAN
TERRITORY

Lake
St. Clair

London

Fort
Detroit

Thames R.

Port
Talbot

Maguaga

Sandwich

Brownstown

Amherstburg

LAKE ERIE

Frenchtown

Point
Pelee

SEAT OF
WAR
1812

Rapids of
the Maumee

Cleveland

Maumee River

Fort Defiance

Sandusky

Tippecanoe R.

Au Glaize

River

Upper
Sandusky

Wabash

INDIANA
TERRITORY

OHIO

Ohio River

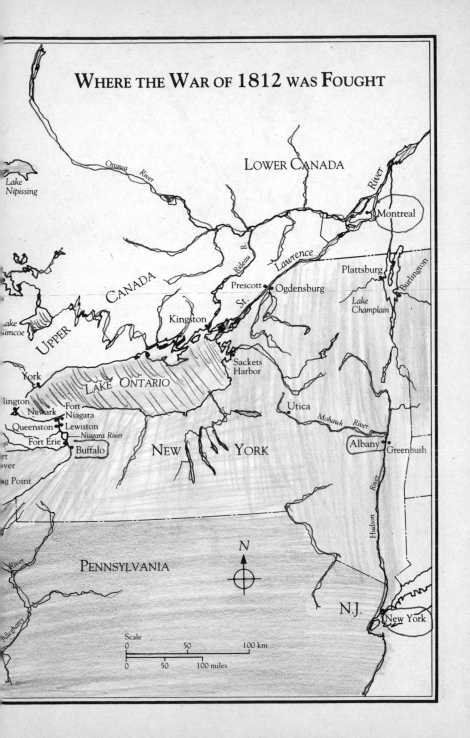

WHERE THE WAR OF 1812 WAS FOUGHT

Lake Nipissing

Ottawa River

LOWER CANADA

River

Montreal

Rideau R.

St. Lawrence

Prescott   Ogdensburg

Plattsburg

Burlington

Kingston

Lake Champlain

CANADA

UPPER

Lake Simcoe

York

Sackets Harbor

LAKE ONTARIO

Burlington

Newark

Fort Niagara

Utica

Mohawk River

Queenston

Lewiston

Niagara River

Albany   Greenbush

Fort Erie

Buffalo

NEW   YORK

River

g Point

Hudson River

N

PENNSYLVANIA

River

N.J.

New York

Alleghany

Scale

0   50   100 km

0   50   100 miles

OVERVIEW

The peculiar war

WHEN WAR BROKE out between the United States and Canada in June of 1812, John Richardson rushed to join the colours. He was only 15 – a slight, curly-headed, clean shaven youth – but, unlike so many of his neighbours, he was eager to serve his country.

Many of his neighbours on the Detroit river were recent arrivals from the United States, reluctant to fight their former compatriots. But Richardson came of solid Canadian stock. His mother's father, John Askin, was a famous fur trader. His grandmother was an Ottawa Indian of the Algonquin nation. And so young John, to his considerable delight, found himself accepted as a "gentleman volunteer" in a regular regiment – the British 41st – stationed in Fort Amherstburg not far from the present site of Windsor. In the next thirty months, he probably saw more of the War of 1812 than any other teenager in Upper Canada.

After fifteen months of fighting, Richardson was captured by the Americans – a capture that tells us a good deal about that most peculiar of wars. Unlike so many prisoners in so many jail cells around the world, he could be fairly sure of decent treatment by his enemies, because he knew so many of them. His grandfather, John Askin, had only to write a note to the American colonel at Fort Detroit asking him to look after the boy. After all, that colonel was Askin's son-in-law. The man in charge of his prison was another relative.

The War of 1812, then, must be seen as a civil war fought by men and women on both sides of a border that all had ignored until hostilities broke out. Many were former neighbours who spoke the same language and were often related to one another. Unlike the Richardsons, three out of every five were former Americans.

Some had come up from the United States after the American Revolution. These "Tories", as their compatriots called them, were fiercely loyal to the British crown. Canadians know them as "United Empire Loyalists." They formed the backbone of the volunteer civilian army, known as the militia.

The others were more recent arrivals. They came to Canada because the land was cheap and taxes almost non-existent. They wanted to be left alone to clear the land of stumps, to drain the marshes, till the soil, and harvest their crops of wheat, barley and corn, or tend the apple, pear and cherry trees that grew so abundantly along the border.

For them, life was hard enough without war. They built their own cabins and barns with the help of their neighbours and, since there was scarcely anything resembling a shop or a store, they made everything themselves, from farm implements to the homespun clothing that was the universal dress. Those villages that existed at all were mere huddles of shacks. Communication was difficult and sometimes impossible. Newspapers were virtually unknown. In the single room schoolhouses, children learned to read, write, and figure – not much more.

These people didn't want to fight any more than their counterparts, the civilian soldiers south of the border. It was indeed a peculiar war that moved along in fits and starts, like a springless buggy bumping over a dirt track. At harvest time and seeding, farmers on both sides deserted or were sent off to tend to their crops. In winter, nothing moved; it was too cold to fight, and so each autumn all activity was postponed until spring.

It was, like so many conflicts, a very silly war. Communication was so bad that hundreds of soldiers, not to mention generals, had no idea it had begun. The last bloody battle was fought long after peace had been declared. The problems that had caused the war in the first place – Great Britain's attacks on American shipping – were solved well before the war ended. But the war went on – men were maimed and killed, farms were vandalized, barns were burned, whole communities put to the torch, and "traitors" hanged for no purpose.

Why were young Canadians like John Richardson fighting young Americans along the international border? The Canadians who fought did so to protect their country from attack. The Americans were fighting for something less tangible – their honour. Once again, they felt, the British were pushing them around. The War of 1812 was in many ways a continuation of the War of Independence fought forty years before. *1772*

It started with Napoleon Bonaparte, the dictator of France. Bonaparte wanted to conquer all of Europe, and so the British found themselves locked in a long and bloody struggle with him – a struggle that began with the great British naval victory at Trafalgar and ended a decade later with the famous battle of Waterloo.

But in their zeal to conquer Napoleon, the British pushed the Americans too far. By boarding American ships on the high seas and kidnapping American sailors for service in the Royal Navy – on the grounds that these seamen were actually British deserters – they got the Americans' backs up. Then, in order to strangle the French by a sea blockade, the British announced they would seize any ship that dared sail directly for a French port. By 1812, they had captured four hundred American vessels, some within sight of the U.S. coast.

That was too much. The United States at last declared war on Great Britain. Since it couldn't attack England directly, it determined to give the British a bloody nose by invading its colony, Canada.

To former President Thomas Jefferson, that seemed "a mere matter of marching." Surely the United States, with a population of eight million, could easily defeat a mere three hundred thousand Canadians!

The odds, however, weren't quite as unequal as Jefferson supposed. Great Britain had 17,000 regular troops stationed in Upper and Lower Canada. The entire U.S. regular army numbered only 7,000, many of them badly trained.

Moreover, the British controlled the water routes – Lakes Huron, Erie and Ontario, and also the St. Lawrence River. For that was the key to both mobility and communication. The roads were almost worthless when they existed at all – not much more than rutted cart tracks. Everything – supplies, troops and weapons – moved by water.

When the war broke out, the Americans were prevented from using this water highway by the presence of the Royal Navy on the lakes. A British express canoe could move swiftly and fearlessly all the way to Lake Superior, carrying dispatches. But the American high command had difficulty communicating at all, which explains why its outposts didn't know for a month that the war was on. The Americans had to use express riders – bold men on horseback, plunging through a jungle of forest and swamp and exposed at every turn to an Indian ambush.

No wonder, then, that almost from the outset the War of 1812 developed into a shipbuilding contest, with both sides feverishly hammering men-of-war to completion in a race to control the lakes.

The Indians were another asset for the British. The

Americans had turned them into enemies, burning their crops and villages and hunting them down like wild animals. In American eyes, the Indians were an obstruction to be pushed aside or eliminated as the pioneers and settlers moved resolutely westward. But the Canadians hadn't fought the Indians since the days of the French-English wars fifty years before. They saw them as harvesters of furs, or, as in the case of the Mohawks of the Grand Valley, loyal subjects of the King. Indians

The American attitude caused John Richardson's boyhood friend, Tecumseh, to move into Upper Canada from the U.S. with his followers to fight on the British side. The native allies numbered no more than 2,000 in all, but with their woodcraft they made a formidable enemy. The Americans were terrified of the Indians. The mere hint that a force of natives was advancing could send a chill through the blood of the citizen soldiers of Ohio or Kentucky.

As a member of the regular army, John Richardson wore a scarlet uniform and carried a musket almost as tall as himself. This awkward, muzzle-loading "Brown Bess" was the basic infantry weapon – and a notoriously inaccurate one. The little one-ounce (.03 kg) ball, wobbling down the smooth barrel, could fly off in any direction. Richardson and his fellow soldiers didn't bother to aim their weapons; they pointed them in the direction of the enemy, waited for the command, and then fired in unison.

The effect of several hundred men, marching in line and in step, shoulders touching, and advancing behind a spray of lead, could be devastating. The noise alone was terrifying. The musket's roar makes the crack of a modern rifle sound like a popgun. Smokeless powder was unknown; after the first volley the battlefield was shrouded in a thick fog of grey.

It required twelve separate movements to load and fire a musket. A well-drilled soldier could get off two or three shots a minute. By that time he was usually close enough to the enemy to rely on his bayonet.

Young Richardson learned to remove a paper cartridge from his pouch, tear off the top with his teeth, pour a little powder in the firing pan and the rest down the barrel. Then he stuffed it with wadding, tapped it tight with his ramrod and dropped in the ball. When he pulled the trigger it engaged the flintlock whose spark (he hoped) would ignite the powder in the pan and send a flash through a pinhole, exploding the charge in the barrel. As Richardson himself discovered at the Battle of Frenchtown later that year, it didn't always work. The phrase "a flash in the pan" comes down to us from those days.

Some of the American woodsmen used the famous Tennessee rifle, a far more accurate weapon because of the spiral groove inside the barrel. That put a spin on the ball – in the same way a pitcher does in baseball – making it far easier to hit the target. However, it was slower to load and was used mainly by snipers or individual soldiers.

A more terrible weapon was the cannon, which operated on the same flintlock principle as the musket. From the tiny three-pounders (1.4 kg) to the big twenty-four-pounders (eleven kg), these weapons were identified by the weight of shot they hurled at the ramparts of the defenders. A sixteen-pound (seven kg) ball of solid pig iron (known as "roundshot") could knock down a file of two dozen men. Bombs – hollowed out shot, crammed with powder and bric-a-brac, and fused to explode in mid-air – were even more devastating. Every soldier feared the canister and grape shot – sacks or metal canisters filled with musket balls that broke apart in the air, sending scores of projectiles whirling above the enemy.

Crude as they seem to us now, these weapons caused a dreadful havoc for the soldiers who fought in the war. Men with mangled limbs and jagged wounds faced searing pain because anaesthetics had not been invented. Yet, grievously wounded men pleaded with army surgeons to amputate a wounded limb as quickly as possible for fear of gangrene. They swallowed a tot of rum or whisky, held a bullet ("biting the bullet") between their gritted teeth, and endured fearful agony as the knives and saws did their work.

Sanitation in the field was primitive, for science had not yet discovered that diseases were caused by germs. Measles, typhus, typhoid, influenza, and dysentery probably put more men out of action than the enemy. The universal remedy was liquor – a daily glass of strong Jamaica rum for the British, a quarter pint (0.2 L) of raw whisky for the Americans. In battle after battle, the combatants on both sides were at least half drunk. Hundreds of youths who had never touched hard liquor in their lives learned to stiffen their resolve through alcohol in the War of 1812.

These were civilian soldiers, members of the militia. In Canada, the Sedentary Militia, largely untrained, was available in times of crisis. Every fit male between 18 and 60 was required to serve in it when needed. Few had uniforms, and those who did were as tattered as beggars. Often they were sent home to their farms after a battle to be called up later.

Some signed up in the Incorporated Militia of Upper Canada for the duration of the war. These were young men inspired by patriotism, a sense of adventure, or the bounty of 80 dollars paid to every volunteer upon enlistment. In Lower Canada, a similar body of the Select Embodied Militia, composed of men between 18 and 25, was drawn by lot to serve for a minimum of two years. They were paid and trained as regular soldiers. In addition some regular units were also recruited in Canada, bearing such names as The Glengarry Fencibles or the Canadian Voltigeurs.

The American draftees and volunteers were engaged by the various states for shorter periods – as little as a month, as much as a year. Most refused to serve beyond that period; few were properly trained. Born of Revolution and dedicated to absolute democracy, the United States had decided against a large standing army. The citizen soldiers even elected their own officers – an awkward and not very efficient process, sneered at by the regulars. And they were recruited to fight *only* in defence of their country.

That caused a major problem for the United States.

Legally, the state militia didn't have to cross the border. Hundreds who had been drafted reluctantly used that excuse when their superiors tried to goad them into attacking Canada. Jefferson had said it was "a mere matter of marching", but when the armies reached the border, the marching stopped.

They didn't want to fight any more than their former compatriots, now tilling the fields and tending the orchards on the other side. That was one of the reasons why this peculiar war ended in stalemate. The Americans derived very little benefit from it; nor did the Indians, who were eventually betrayed by both sides when the peace talks were held. The only real victors were the Canadians, who got no territory but gained something less tangible, yet in the end more precious. Having helped to hurl back five American armies, the plain people who had once been so indifferent to the war developed both a sense of pride and a sense of community. They had come through the fire and they had survived. In a very real sense the War of 1812 marked the first faint stirrings of a united Canadian nation.

CHAPTER ONE
Isaac Brock's secret message

THERE WAS A TIME, at the turn of the nineteenth century, when the city of Detroit was nothing more than a palisaded fort in the wilderness. Windsor did not yet exist, except in the village of Sandwich, now a Windsor suburb. A few kilometres down the Detroit river, as it enters Lake Erie, was the British Fort Amherstburg, which the Americans called Fort Malden. And it was here that the War of 1812 began.

It was from Fort Detroit that the Americans hoped to invade Canada in the summer of 1812. It seemed simple enough. The British fort was lightly held and a large American force of 2,200 men was advancing toward the border. But, as it turned out, it wasn't simple at all. Instead of surrendering to superior numbers, the Canadians, British, and Indians turned the tables on the invaders and seized not only Fort Detroit but most of Michigan Territory with scarcely a drop of blood spilled.

How did they do it? How did they capture an entire American army? The answer has less to do with soldiers

and guns than with the personalities of the two opposing commanders, the British general, Isaac Brock, who hated and despised his job, and his American opposite number, William Hull, an old soldier who didn't really want to fight.

Both had a long experience of war, but Hull at 58 was in decline while Brock, a vibrant 42, was fairly itching for battle.

It tells you something about Hull that his men thought him closer to 70. As Governor of Michigan Territory, he saw himself as a father figure, protecting his people from the ravages of the Indians who had been driven to the British side by American policies. Certainly, he looked like a grandfather with his distinguished features gone to flesh, and his shock of dead white hair. He chewed tobacco unceasingly, especially when he was nervous; then his jaws worked overtime.

During the American Revolution, Hull had been a bold and gallant officer who fought with distinction, survived nine battles, and received the official thanks of Congress. But now he was fading away.

Brock, on the other hand, breathed hell-fire. Let us look at him a few months before the war – the date is February 27 – seated in his study in Little York, the future site of Toronto, composing a secret letter that will affect the future of his country. We see a remarkably handsome soldier with a fair complexion, a broad forehead, clear eyes of grey blue and sparkling white teeth. Isaac Brock fitted the kind of role that Hollywood casting directors have in mind when they need an actor to play a British officer.

He was a massive figure, was Brock, big boned and powerful, almost six foot, three inches (two m) in height, with a slight tendency to portliness and the flush of middle age on his cheeks. But in his own words – and his own words survive in his letters and documents – he was "hard as nails." He was popular, too – especially with his soldiers – but he was also aloof. He took few into his confidence.

Behind that formidable exterior there was concealed a frustrated soul. Brock was the most powerful man in Upper Canada; president and chief administrator of the province and head of the army – a virtual dictator, in short, who took his orders from the Governor General in Montreal. But he was not happy. He wanted desperately to be in on the *real* fighting – in Europe where the Duke of Wellington was locked in a life and death struggle with Napoleon's armies.

Brock didn't care for Canada. To him it was a frontier backwater, especially York, which he found as unsophisticated as it was muddy. A gourmet, a lover of fine wines, an omnivorous reader, and a spirited dancer at society balls, he longed for a larger community. He despised the local legislature and was quite prepared to ride over it roughshod if necessary. General Brock was no democrat. Democracy to him was an American concept – and a poisonous one.

Now, in this very month of February, he had been handed exactly what he desired – permission from the Governor General to escape from his colonial prison and join Welling-

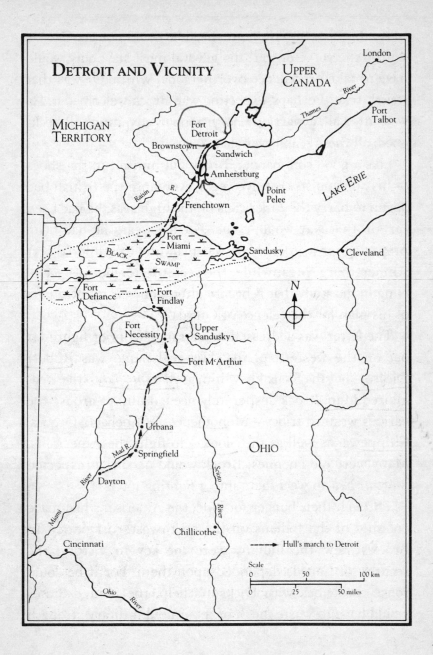

DETROIT AND VICINITY

UPPER CANADA

London

MICHIGAN TERRITORY

Fort Detroit

Brownstown

Sandwich

Amherstburg

Port Talbot

Thames River

LAKE ERIE

Racin R.

Point Pelee

Frenchtown

Fort Miami

BLACK SWAMP

Sandusky

Cleveland

Fort Defiance

Fort Findlay

N

Fort Necessity

Upper Sandusky

Fort McArthur

Urbana

Mad R.

Springfield

OHIO

Scioto River

Miami River

Dayton

Chillicothe

Cincinnati

- - - ► Hull's march to Detroit

Scale

| 0 | | 50 | | 100 km |

| 0 | 25 | | 50 miles |

Ohio River

25

ton in Europe. Bitterly, he realized he could not go. Canada was on the verge of war; the general must stay; duty would have to take precedence over personal whim. Or was that strictly true? Perhaps, expecting war, Brock welcomed it. He was, after all, a warrior. Glory, honour, adventure all beckoned; all these – and even death.

Like a good commander, Brock put himself in the shoes of his antagonists. For five years, ever since the British had begun to harry the Americans on the high seas, he had been certain that war would come. For five years he had been preparing for it. Already he was planning to reinforce Fort Amherstburg. Meanwhile, the secret letter he was scribbling in his study that February afternoon was to form part of his plan for the defence of Canada.

The letter was addressed to a strange frontier figure far out on the western plains. His real name was Robert Dickson, but the Sioux knew him as *Mascotopah* – the Red-Haired Man. Brock desperately needed him to arouse the various western tribes – Menomenee, Winnebago, Ottawa, Chippewa, as well as the Sioux – to fight the Americans. Many were old enemies; Brock would need the respected *Mascotopah* to weld them into a fighting force.

Through their hunger for land, the Americans had made enemies of the Indians on the northwestern frontier. In Brock's view, the Indians were the key to victory; the security of Canada depended upon them. For if he could rouse the tribes with Dickson's help, the United States would have to waste much of its limited military strength trying to subdue them. That would weaken the invading army.

This was the substance of his secret communication. Dickson was born a Scot but he was as close to being an Indian as any white could be. His wife was the sister of a Sioux chief. His domain covered the present day states of Iowa, Wisconsin and Minnesota.

Dickson was out there somewhere in that empty wilderness, nobody knew quite where – a white man living like an Indian and exercising all the powers of a Sioux chief. Brock had to find him before the war began and that would not be easy.

He knew that the Indians would fight the Americans only if they were convinced the British were winning. If he could seize the American island of Michilimackinac, he knew the tribes would take heart.

This little rock was immensely significant and, if you look at the map, you will see why. It sits in the channel which joins three of the Great Lakes – Michigan, Superior, and Huron. Any force entering any of these lakes would have to come under its guns. If Dickson and his followers could seize it, they would control the water highway of the north west.

Isaac Brock believed that offence is the best defence. If Mackinac fell, then Dickson's Indians would help him attack Detroit. There, they would be joined by another native force – those disenchanted members of several American tribes who had come together under the great Shawnee war chief, Tecumseh, to do battle on the British side. And if Detroit

American

fell, more Indians would join – even, he hoped, the Mo-hawks who, to this time, had been distressingly neutral.

And so he sent off his secret missive addressed only: "To Mr. Robert Dickson residing with the Indians near Mis-souri." Almost five months went by before he received his answer, an answer that was already outdated by events. Long before that, the Red-Haired Man and his friends, anticipa-ting Brock, had departed for Canada to prepare for the invasion of the unsuspecting island.

CHAPTER TWO
The Americans march north

BROCK WAS DEAD RIGHT. It was the Indians who dictated Washington's plans in a war that was not yet declared. Tecumseh and his followers were creating chaos in the Indiana and Michigan territories. The United States would have to deal with them before attacking Montreal.

To advance the American war plans, the administration invited William Hull, the Governor of Michigan Territory, to come to Washington, to discuss the defence of the northwestern frontier. Washington believed in Hull. Because he had a reputation for sound judgment, personal courage, and decisive command, President Madison listened carefully to his advice.

Hull pointed out that the United States must secure Lake Erie by reinforcing the tiny fort at Detroit and by building warships to command the water routes. Only in that way could they be sure of the swift movement of men and supplies.

Hull realized, as Brock did, that the Indians held the key to defeat or victory. A formidable army at Detroit, denying

the lake to British ships, could cut the Indians off from the British and perhaps prevent a general uprising of the tribes. Hull was convinced that without the Indians "the British cannot hold Upper Canada."

The government agreed, and Hull was told to raise an army of twelve hundred volunteers from the Ohio Militia. With that force he would have to cut a road through forest and swamp for two hundred miles (320 km) from Urbana, Ohio, to Detroit, and thus secure the frontier.

It all made sense on paper. But it depended on inspired leadership, swift communications, careful timing, well trained troops, an efficient war department, and a united, enthusiastic nation. Unfortunately for the Americans, none of these conditions existed.

The men seemed anxious enough to fight. By May, Ohio's quota of twelve hundred volunteers was over-subscribed. Sixteen hundred answered the call. The new general joined his troops at Dayton, Ohio, after a journey that left him weak from cold and fever. In spite of his reputation, he was a flabby old soldier, tired of war, hesitant of command, and suspicious of the militia who he knew were untrained and suspected were untrustworthy.

He paraded his troops on May 25 – an unruly lot, noisy, disobedient, untrained. He was appalled. Their arms were unfit for use, the leather covering the cartridge boxes was rotten, many had no blankets or clothing. No armourers had been provided to repair the weapons, no means adopted to furnish the missing clothing; no stores of arms or supplies existed. The powder in the magazines was useless. America wasn't ready for battle. It hadn't contemplated an offensive war – or even a defensive one – at any time since the Revolution.

When Hull and his staff set off to view the troops with a fife and drum corps leading the way, there was a note of farce. The sound of the drums frightened the ponies. The General's horse shied. Hull's feet slipped out of the stirrups, he lost his balance, his hat flew off, and he was forced to cling to the animal's mane in a most unsoldierly fashion until it slowed to a walk. It was not a happy beginning for the invasion of Canada.

The volunteers were formed into three regiments. Because they elected their own leaders, their officers had to act as politicians. In fact the three regimental commanders had been politicians in civilian life. Hull had his trouble with these three, one of whom called him "a weak old man." Hull was just as contemptuous of the volunteers as they were of him.

The army started to march north on June 1. A few days later at the frontier community of Urbana, the last outpost of civilization, Hull's suspicions were reinforced. From that point to Detroit the troops faced two hundred miles (320 km) of wilderness with no pathway, not even an Indian trail to follow. The volunteers turned ugly. They had been promised an advance of fifty dollars each for a year's clothing; they got only sixteen. They rode one unpopular officer out of camp on a rail and, when the orders came to march, scores refused to move. Only the regular infantry was able to prod the wavering volunteers into action.

Off they went, hacking away through jungle and forest, as much a mob as an army. The rain fell all the time. The newly-built road became a swamp. Wagons were mired and had to be hoisted by brute strength. The troops kept their spirits up on corn liquor supplied by friendly settlers.

They plunged through the pelting rain into the no man's land of the Black Swamp, a labyrinth of deadfalls and ghostly trees behind whose trunks Tecumseh's unseen Indian spies kept watch. A fog of insects clogged the soldiers' nostrils and bloated their faces; a gruel of mud and water rotted their boots and swelled their ankles. They could not rest at day's end until they hacked out a barricade against Indian attack.

Strung out for two miles (3.2 km), day after day, the human serpent finally wriggled to a halt, blocked by rising water and unbridgeable streams. Hull camped his men in ankle-deep mud, and built a blockhouse: which he named Fort Necessity. There, the sodden army waited until the floods ebbed. Yet Hull himself was not cast down. He had more than two thousand rank and file under his command and still believed his force superior to any that might oppose it.

The troops finally moved out and reached a branch of the Maumee River. And there a letter caught up with Hull from the Secretary of War urging him to advance with all possible haste to Fort Detroit, to await further orders. That letter was dated June 18. It must have been written on the morning of that day, because it failed to include the one piece of information essential to prevent a major blunder.

On the afternoon of June 18, the United States officially declared war on Great Britain.

CHAPTER THREE
The Red-Haired Man

O N THE VERY DAY that war was declared, Brock's courier
caught up at last with the Red-Haired Man. He found
him at the Wisconsin-Fox portage in Illinois territory.
Robert Dickson was a man of commanding presence, a
massive and cheerful six-footer (two m), with a flaming
shock of red hair and ruddy face to match. Everybody liked
him. There was an easy sociability about Dickson – a
dignity, a sense of honour and principle. Men of every colour
trusted him. He was also humane. He had tried to teach the
Indians not to kill and scalp when they took prisoners. The
greatest warriors, he told his people, were those who saved
their captives rather than destroyed them.

What was he doing out here in this lonely land? He lived
often in great squalor, existing for weeks on wild rice, corn,
and pemmican or sometimes on nothing but melted snow,
going for months without hearing his native tongue, trudg-
ing for kilometres on snowshoes or struggling over long
portages with back-breaking loads; he was never at rest. He

knew no real home but moved ceaselessly along his string of trading posts like a trapper tending a trap line.

His two brothers, who also emigrated from Scotland, preferred the civilized life. But Robert Dickson had spent twenty years in Indian country. Why? Certainly not for profit. He had little money; the fur trade was a risky business. Not for glory, for there was no glory. For power? He could have had more in the white man's world. The answer seems to be that he was here, like so many of his countrymen, for the adventure of the frontier – the risks, the dangers, the excitement, and now, perhaps, because after two decades these were his people, and this wild, untravelled land was his home. Beyond the Great Lakes there were others like him, living among the Indians, exploring the land. Most were Scotsmen.

Dickson liked the Indians for themselves. He was faithful to his Indian wife, prided himself that he was educating his half Indian children, and was angered by the treatment his people received from American frontiersmen who saw the Indian as a dangerous animal to be exterminated. His patriotism needed no fuelling. He was more than delighted to aid his countrymen.

He lost no time. That very day he sent a reply to Brock and dispatched it to Fort Amherstburg with thirty Menomenee warriors. Then with one hundred and thirty Sioux, Winnebago, and Menomenee, he set off for St. Joseph's Island, the British outpost at the western entrance to Lake Huron. There he waited for orders.

They came by express canoe on July 15. The British commander at St. Joseph's Island, Captain Charles Roberts, was told to "adopt the most prudent measure either of offence or defence which circumstances might point out." Roberts resolved to make the most of these ambiguous instructions. The following morning to the skirl of fife and the roll of drum – banners waving, Indians whooping – his polyglot army embarked upon the glassy waters of the lake.

Off sailed the gunboat *Caledonia* (seized from the Montreal-based North West fur trading company), loaded with two brass cannon, her decks bright with the red tunics of the forty regulars. Behind her followed ten big square-prowed bateaux crammed with one hundred and eighty voyageurs, brilliant in their sashes, silk kerchiefs, and capotes. Slipping in and out of the flotilla were seventy painted birchbark canoes containing close to three hundred tribesmen – Dickson, in Indian dress, with fifty feathered Sioux; their one-time enemies, the Chippewa, with coal black faces, shaved heads and bodies daubed with pipe clay; two dozen Winnebago, including the celebrated one-eyed chief, Big Canoe; forty Menomenee under their head chief, Tomah; and thirty Ottawa led by Amable Chevalier, the half-white trader whom they recognized as leader.

Ahead lay the Island of Michilimackinac (known simply as Mackinac and pronounced "Mackinaw"). Shaped like an aboriginal arrowhead, it was almost entirely surrounded by 150 foot (45 m) cliffs of soft grey limestone. The British had abandoned it grudgingly following the Revolution, though they realized its strategic importance. Control of Mackinac meant control of the western fur trade. No wonder Roberts had no trouble conscripting Canadian voyageurs.

They were pulling on their oars like madmen, for they had to reach their objective, some fifty miles (eighty km) to the south west, well before dawn. Around midnight, about fifteen miles (24 km) from the island, they spotted a birchbark canoe. Its passenger was an old crony from Mackinac, a Pennsylvania fur trader named Michael Dousman. He was sent by Porter Hanks, the American commander, to try to find out what was taking place north of the border.

Dousman, in spite of the fact that he was an American militia commander, was first and foremost a fur trader, and an old colleague and an occasional partner of the leaders of the voyageurs and Indians. He greeted Dickson and the others as old friends, and cheerfully told Roberts everything he needed to know: the strength of the American garrison, its armament (or lack of it), and – most important of all – the fact that no one on the island had been told that America was at war.

Dousman's and Roberts's concerns were identical. In the event of a struggle they wanted to protect the civilians on the island from the wrath of the Indians. Dousman agreed to wake the village quietly and herd everybody into the old distillery at the end of town where they could be guarded by the detachment of regulars. He promised not to warn the garrison.

Chapter Four
Bloodless victory

A<small>T MICHILIMACKINAC THE</small> Americans slept. The lake was silent in those small hours – silent save for the whisper of waves lapping the shoreline. In the starlight, the island's cliffs stood out darkly against the surrounding flatland. In the fort above the village at the southern tip the American commander, Lieutenant Hanks, lay asleep, ignorant of a war that would tragically affect his future. It was nine months since he had heard from Washington. For all he knew of the civilized world he might as well be on the moon.

The civilized world ended at the Detroit River, some 350 miles (560 km) to the southeast. Mackinac Island was its outpost, lying in the narrows between Lakes Huron and Michigan. Whoever controlled it controlled the routes to the fur country – the domain of the Nor'Westers, beyond Superior and the no man's land of the Upper Missouri and Mississippi. It was a prize worth fighting for.

Hanks slumbered on, oblivious of the quiet bustling in the village directly below – of low knockings, whispers, small children's cries quickly hushed, rustlings, soft footsteps, the

41

creak of cartwheels on grass – slumbered fitfully, his dreams troubled by a growing uneasiness, until the drum roll of reveille woke him.

At three that morning the British had landed on a small beach facing the only break in the escarpment at the north end of the island. With the help of Dousman's ox team the voyageurs managed to drag the two six-pounders (three kg) over the boulders and through thickets up to the 300-foot (ninety m) crest that overlooked the fort at the southern tip. Meanwhile Dousman had tiptoed from door to door waking the inhabitants, silently herding them to safety.

When Hanks woke, he peered over the palisades at the fort and gazed down at the village below, a crescent of whitewashed houses, following the curve of a pebbled beach. He saw at once that something was wrong because the village was not sleeping; it was dead. No curl of smoke rose above the cedarbark roofs; no human cry echoed across the waters of the lake; no movement ruffled the weeds that edged the roadway.

What was going on? He ordered his second in command, Lieutenant Archibald Darragh, to find out, but he did not need to wait for Darragh's report. Clambering up a slope was the surgeon's mate, Sylvester Day, who preferred to live in the village. Dr. Day's breathless report was blunt: British Redcoats and Indians had landed. The villagers had been herded into an old distillery at the west end of town. Three of the most prominent citizens were under guard as hostages.

Hanks reacted instantly. He mustered his men, stocked his blockhouses with ammunition, charged his field pieces, and followed the book. He must have known that he was merely playing soldier, for he had fewer than sixty effective troops under his command – men made stale by their frontier exile. Presently he became aware of a British six-pounder on the forested bluff above pointing directly into his bastion. Through the spring foliage he could see the flash of British scarlet and – the ultimate horror – the dark forms of their native allies. A single word formed in his mind, a truly terrible word for anyone with frontier experience; *massacre* – visions of mutilated bodies, decapitated children, disembowelled housewives, scalps bloodying the pickets.

Hanks could fight to the last man and become a hero – after his death. If it were merely the aging troops of St. Joseph's that faced him, he might be prepared to do just that, but to the last woman? To the last child? Against an enemy whose savagery was said to be without limits?

A white flag fluttered before him. Under its protection a British truce party marched into the fort, accompanied by the three civilian hostages. The parley was brief and to the point. Hanks must surrender. The accompanying phrase "or else" hung unspoken in the air. The hostages urged him to accept, but it is doubtful whether he needed their counsel. He agreed to everything. The fort and island would become British. The Americans would have to take the oath of allegiance to the King or leave. The troops were to be paroled to their homes. That meant that they promised to take no further part in the war until exchanged with prisoners from the other side.

The war? *What* war? The date was July 17. A full month had passed since the United States declared war on Great Britain but this was the first Hanks had heard of it. Nobody in Washington seemed to have seen the urgency of a speedy warning to the western flank on the American frontier. It was typical of this senseless and tragic conflict that it should begin in this topsy-turvy fashion, with the invaders invaded in a trackless wilderness hundreds of miles from the nerve centre of command.

For that oversight the American government would pay dearly. This bloodless battle was also one of the most significant. The news of the capture of Michilimackinac Island touched off a chain of events that frustrated the Americans in their attempt to seize British North America.

And so the first objective in Isaac Brock's carefully programmed campaign to frustrate invasion had been taken without firing a shot. "It is a circumstance I believe without precedent," Roberts reported to Brock. And for the Indians' white leaders he had special praise. Their influence with the tribes was such "that as soon as they heard capitulation was signed they all returned to the Canoes, not one drop either of Man's or Animal's blood was Spilt. . . ." Hanks's bloodless surrender had prevented a massacre.

Dickson's Indians felt cheated out of a fight. They complained to the Red-Haired Man who kept them firmly under control, explaining that Americans could not be killed once they surrendered. To placate them he turned loose a number of cattle which were chased around the island, their flanks bristling with arrows until they hurled themselves into the water. They were further appeased by a distribution of blankets, provisions, and guns taken from the American military stores. There, they also found tonnes of pork and flour, a vast quantity of vinegar, soap, candles, and – to the delight of everybody – 357 gallons (1,600 L) of high wines and 253 gallons (630 L) of whisky, enough to get every man, white and red, so drunk that had an enemy of force appeared on the lake it might easily have recaptured the island.

In addition to these spoils a treasure of government-owned furs brought the total of captured goods to 10,000 pounds sterling, all of it to be distributed according to custom among the regulars and volunteers who captured the fort. Every private soldier eventually received ten pounds as his share of the prize money, the officers considerably more.

The message to the Indians was clear: America was a weak nation and rewards could be gained in fighting for the British. The fall of Mackinac gave the British the entire control of the tribes of the Old Northwest.

Porter Hanks and his men were sent off to Detroit under parole. They gave their word not to take any further part in the war until they were exchanged for British or Canadian soldiers of equivalent rank captured by the Americans. This method was used throughout the conflict to eliminate the need for large camps of prisoners to be fed and clothed at the enemy's expense. The Americans who stayed on the island were obliged to take an oath of allegiance to the Crown; otherwise they must return to American territory. Most found it easy to switch sides, since they had done it before. A good many were originally British until the island changed hands in 1796.

CHAPTER FIVE
Prisoners of the British

LIKE PORTER HANKS, General William Hull's tattered army did not know that war had been declared, as they trudged doggedly toward Detroit. At the foot of the Maumee Rapids, Hull was able to relieve his exhausted teams by loading the schooner *Cuyahoga* with all his excess military stores – uniforms, band instruments, entrenching tools, personal luggage – and some thirty-six officers and men, together with three women who had somehow managed to keep up with their husbands through the long trek north.

That was foolish. War was clearly imminent even though Hull, marching on to Detroit, had no word about it. His own officers pointed out that the *Cuyahoga* would have to pass under the British guns at Fort Amherstburg – guns that were guarding the narrow river boundary – before she could reach Detroit. But their commander, sublimely unaware of his country's declaration, remained confident that the vessel would get to Detroit before the British army.

Hull's assistant quartermaster-general, an observant soldier named William K. Beall, stretched out on the deck

admiring the view of Lake Erie. Beall was the kind of man who notes everything and writes it all down. It's from men and women like him that we can gain a picture of the past. He was a prosperous Kentucky plantation owner who had never beheld so much fresh water stretching beyond the horizon. The only water he had seen since leaving home had flowed sluggishly in saffron streams veining the dreadful swamps through which the army had just toiled.

As the schooner approached Amherstburg, the little town nestled outside the British fort, Beall was charmed by the view of sunny wheat fields rippling in the breeze. This southern fringe of orchards was the garden of Upper Canada, but most of the province beyond remained a wilderness, its great forests of pine and oak, maple and basswood broken here and there by small patches of pioneer civilization, like worn spots on a rug. Today Amherstburg is a flourishing town – almost a suburb of Windsor.

Vast swamps, dark and terrifying, smothered the land. Roads were few and, in some seasons, impassable. Sensible travellers moved by water, and it was along the margins of the lake and the banks of the larger river that the main communities such as Amherstburg had sprung up. Between these villages lay smaller settlements. Plots of winter wheat, oats, and rye, fields of corn and vegetables blurred the edges of the forest. Here, along the Detroit River, fruit trees had been bearing for a decade and cider had become a staple drink.

To Beall everything appeared to wear "the cheering

smiles of peace and plenty." In the distance he spotted a picturesque Indian canoe. But, as the canoe came closer, it was transformed into a Canadian longboat commanded by an officer of the provincial marine, Lieutenant Frederic Rolette, with six seamen, armed with cutlasses and pistols, pulling on the oars.

Rolette called to *Cuyahoga*'s captain, Luther Chapin, to lower his mainsails. Chapin was open mouthed. He'd expected a friendly hail, but now he saw six muskets raised against him. Before he could act, Rolette fired his pistol in the air. Chapin struggled with a sail. Beall and his fellow passengers were in confusion. What was happening? Beall ordered the captain to hoist the sail and press on, but Chapin replied that was not possible.

Rolette now pointed his pistol directly at young George Gooding, a second lieutenant in charge of the soldiers and baggage.

"Douse your mainsails!" Rolette ordered. Gooding hesitated.

"I have no command here, sir!" he shouted. Rolette fired directly at the schooner, the ball whistling past Beall's head. Captain Chapin pleaded for instructions.

"Do as you please," answered the rattled Gooding whose wife was also on deck. As the mainsails tumbled, Rolette boarded the packet.

He was astonished to find the decks jammed with American soldiers. They weren't aware the war had started, but Rolette couldn't be sure of that. Nor did he know that all but three were ill, their muskets and ammunition out of reach in the hold. He did know, however, that he was outnumbered five to one.

That did not dismay him. He was a seasoned seaman accustomed to acts of boldness and decision. At the age of twenty-nine, this French-speaking Quebecker had a record any officer might envy. He had fought in the two greatest sea battles of the era – the Nile and Trafalgar – under the finest commander of his time, Horatio Nelson. He had been wounded five times, and before this newest contest was over he would be wounded again. Now he informed the astonished American soldiers that the war was on.

Losing no time, he ordered everybody below decks and posted sentries at the hatches and arms chests with orders to shoot any man who approached them. He told the helmsman to steer the ship under the cannons of Amherstburg and the band to play "God Save the King."

After the schooner had docked, the British realized the importance of their prize. For here they discovered two trunks belonging to General Hull containing documents of extraordinary value. Hull's aide-de-camp – his son Abraham – had foolishly packed the General's personal papers with his baggage. The astonished British found that they now possessed all the details of the army that was opposing them: field states, complete statistics of the troops, names and strengths of their regiments, an incomplete draft of Hull's strategy, all his correspondence to and from the American Secretary of War. It was a find equal to the breaking of an enemy code. The entire package was sent to Brock at York who grasped its significance at once and laid his own plans.

But no one was quite certain how to behave. Had war actually come? Even the British were reluctant to believe it, and William Beall, now a prisoner, doubted it. He was sure his captors were wrongly informed and that, when Hull demanded his return, he and his companions would be permitted to go on to Detroit.

The British were polite, even hospitable. Beall's opposite number in the British quartermaster department, Lieutenant Edward Dewar, urged the Americans not to think of themselves as prisoners, but merely detainees. It was all very unpleasant, Dewar murmured. He hoped the report of the war might prove incorrect. He hoped the Americans would be able to spend their time in detention as agreeably as possible. If there was any service he and his fellow officers could render, he would be pleased to do so. He wished the schooner had been allowed by without interruption. And if they got authentic information that the war had not been declared, the prisoners would be released at once.

Having accepted the parole of the Americans (that they wouldn't try to escape), Dewar invited them to his home where there was wine, cider, and biscuits. The Lieutenant remarked that it would be improper to invite the Americans to dine with them, but he took them to Boyle's Inn and Public House for dinner. Then the men left the inn and strolled through the streets through crowds of Indians.

Every white man bowed politely to the strangers, and one even invited them into his house and poured them several glasses of wine.

Many of the citizens of Amherstburg were new arrivals in Upper Canada who had little interest in politics or war. They formed part of a clear but powerless majority in a province of sixty thousand, having been shut out of all public office by the élite group of British and Loyalist administrators who controlled the government. That didn't concern them because they were prospering on their free acreage. Democracy might be virtually nonexistent in Upper Canada, but so were taxes since the province was financed by the British treasury. As for the prospect of the war, they dismissed that. Everyone echoed that sentiment.

The captured American women, being non-combatants, were sent to the American side; the men remained aboard a British ship, the *Thames*. Beall estimated that there were at least five hundred Indians in Amherstburg. On July 4, as the sounds of the Independence Day cannonades echoed across the water from Detroit, two hundred Sauk warriors arrived – the largest and best formed men that Beall had ever seen. On the following day, the sound of Hull's bugler blowing reveille revealed that the Army of the Northwest had reached the village of Brownstown directly across the river, less than a day's march from Detroit.

By nightfall Amherstburg was in a panic. Women and children ran crying towards the vessels at the dockside, loading the decks with trunks and valuables. Indians dashed about the streets shouting. Consternation and dismay prevailed as the call to arms was sounded. The enemy, in short, was in striking distance of the thinly guarded fort, the sole British bastion on the Detroit frontier. If Hull could seize it in one lightning move then his army could sweep up the valley of the Thames and capture most if not all of Upper Canada.

USA Beall viewed all that with mixed feelings. He was a sensitive and compassionate man, and he was already starting to pine for his wife, Melinda, back in Kentucky. He felt "sensibly for those on both sides who might loose (sic) their lives." His British hosts had been decent to the point of chivalry, and it was difficult to look at them as enemies. On the other hand, he was convinced that his day of deliverance was at hand. Surely General Hull would cross the river, crush all resistance at Amherstburg, free him from further service and, if the campaign was as decisive as everyone expected, then he would return swiftly to Melinda's arms.

CHAPTER SIX
Invasion!

M EANWHILE, ON THE American side all was confusion. The crucial dispatch from Washington to General Hull announcing the declaration of war was hidden somewhere in the Cleveland mail. The postmaster had written orders to forward it at once, but nobody could find it. (In those days, too, they had problems with the mail!) Everybody could guess what it contained because the news had already reached Cleveland.

A young Cleveland lawyer, Charles Shaler, stood ready to gallop through swamp and forest to the rapids of the Maumee and on to Detroit if necessary once the missing document was found. Apparently nobody thought to send him off at once with a verbal message while the others rummaged for the official one. Finally someone suggested the dispatch might be in the Detroit mail, so reluctantly the postmaster broke the law, opened the bags, and found it.

Off went Shaler, swimming the unbridged rivers, plunging through the wilderness, vainly seeking a relay steed to replace his gasping horse. Some eighty hours later, on the

evening of July 1, he reached the rapids to discover the army had decamped and galloped on after it. He reached it at two the following morning.

General Hull, half dressed, read the dispatch, registered alarm, ordered Shaler to keep quiet, called a council of officers and ordered a boat to take after the *Cuyahoga* . He was too late, of course. The army moved on, Shaler riding with the troops. When he reached Detroit his horse dropped dead of exhaustion as a result of the frantic journey.

The army arrived at Detroit on July 5 after thirty-five days of struggle through Ohio's swampy wilderness. Today, it is one of the largest cities in the United States – "Motown" to many. But the soldiers found a primitive settlement of only twelve hundred straggling on the outskirts of a log fort. Like their neighbours on both sides of the river, most were French-speaking, descendants of families that settled on the land a century before and whose strip farms with their narrow river frontage showed their Quebecois background. Some of their descendants remain there today – on both sides of the river. Hull thought they were "miserable farmers" – people with no agricultural tradition. They raised apples for cider and gigantic pears for pickling, but they paid little attention to other forms of agriculture, depending principally on hunting, fishing, and trading with the Indians. In short, they couldn't provision his troops.

That was Hull's dilemma. His supply line was two hundred miles (320 km) long, stretching south along the makeshift trail his men had hacked out of the forests. To secure his position he would have to have two months' provisions. An express rider took the news to the Governor of Ohio, who immediately raised a company of citizen volunteers and sent them north to escort a brigade of pack horses loaded with flour and provisions, and a drove of beef cattle. But to reach Hull's army they would have to follow the road that hugged the southwestern shore of Lake Erie and the Detroit River. That would be dangerous because the British controlled the water.

Meanwhile Hull was concerned about the fate of the baggage captured aboard the *Cuyahoga*. Had the British actually rifled his personal possessions and discovered his official correspondence? He sent a polite and studiedly casual letter to the commander at Fort Amherstburg, Lieutenant-Colonel Thomas Bligh St. George, who told him in equally polite words to go to hell.

But St. George was a badly rattled commander. He was an old campaigner with forty years of service in the British Army, much of it spent in active warfare in the Mediterranean. But he had been a staff officer for the last ten years, and clearly he had difficulty coping with the present crisis. He commanded a lightly garrisoned fort that needed repairs and reinforcements. Across the river an army of two thousand sat poised for invasion. Scrambling about in a fever of preparation he was "so harassed for these five days and nights, I can scarcely write." Brock, who got his letter, was dismayed to discover that St. George had let three days slip by before bothering to tell him that the American army had reached Detroit.

Meanwhile Fort Amherstburg was still in chaos. Indians were coming and going, eating up the supplies. Nobody could guess how many they were from day to day. The same was true of the militia. St. George had no real idea of how many men he commanded or whether he had the resources to feed them. His accounts were in disarray. And he didn't have enough officers to organize the militia. Many were leaving for home or trying to leave. There weren't enough arms to supply them, and he didn't know how he could pay them.

The little village of Sandwich lay directly across the river from Detroit. That, St. George realized, would be Hull's invasion point. He stationed some militia units at Sandwich, but he had little hope they would be effective. In order to study their movements he sent a detachment of regulars. To supply the wants of this confused and amateur army, he had to make use of everything that fell in his way. That included a brigade of eleven bateaux loaded with supplies that the North West Company had sent from Montreal to Fort William at the lake head. St. George seized these, and impressed the seventy voyageurs.

On the docks and the streets the Indians performed war dances, leaping and capering before the doors of the inhabitants who gave them presents of whiskey. William Beall, still captive aboard the *Thames*, noted in his diary that he had seen "the great Tecumseh" whom he described as "a very plane man, rather above middle-size, stout built, a noble set of features and an admirable eye. He is always accompanied by Six great chiefs who never go before him. The women and men all fear that in the event of Genl. Hull's crossing and proving successful, that the Indians being naturally treacherous will turn against them to murder and destroy them."

To the whites, the Indians were "murdering savages." To the Indians, the whites were just as bad. Certainly the frontiersmen of Ohio, Kentucky, and Tennessee were as savage as any native. Memories of the Battle of Tippecanoe, in 1811, still rankled among Tecumseh's mixed band of followers. His village, at the junction of the Tippecanoe and Wabash rivers, had been destroyed by a force of regulars and militiamen under a future U.S. president, William Henry Harrison. Harrison, then governor of Indiana Territory, was greedy for Indian land and determined to shatter Tecumseh's dream of an Indian confederacy stretching from Florida to Lake Erie. And so the Shawnee war chief, with several hundred natives from half a dozen American tribes, had gone over to the British in the vain hope that they would help him achieve his goal.

"Here is a chance presented to us," he said, " – a chance such as will never occur again for us Indians of North America to form themselves into one great combination and cast our lot with the British in this war."

Tecumseh's followers had shadowed Hull's army all the

way through Michigan Territory, warned by their leader to take no overt action before war was declared and he could bring his federation into alliance with Great Britain. Hull had done his best to neutralize them, sending messages to a council at Fort Wayne, promising protection and friendship if the Indians would stay out of the white man's war.

But Tecumseh refused: "I have taken sides with the King, my father, and I will suffer my bones to bleach upon this shore before I recross that stream to join in any council of neutrality."

Upriver at Detroit, Hull prepared to invade Canada by landing his army at Sandwich. He tried to move on July 10 but, to his dismay, discovered that hundreds of militiamen, urged on in some cases by their officers, invoked their constitutional right and refused to cross the river to fight on foreign soil.

Hull tried again the following day. Two companies refused to enter the boats. One finally gave in, but the other stood firm. Hull threw around words like "coward" and "traitor" but to no avail. The crossing was again aborted.

At Sandwich across the river (now a suburb of present day Windsor), an equally reluctant body of citizen soldiers – the militia of Kent and Essex counties, only recently called to service – all sat and waited. They had little if any training, militia service being mainly an excuse for carousing. They weren't eager to fight, especially in midsummer with the winter wheat ripening in the fields. Patriotism had no meaning for most of them; that was the exclusive property of the Loyalists. Most were passively pro-American, having moved up from the border states. Isolated on the scattered farms, they had no sense of a larger community. They learned of the war through handbills. They didn't really care whether or not Upper Canada became another state of the American Union.

Lieutenant-Colonel St. George, convinced that they would flee to their homes at the first shot, decided to get them out of the way before the attack was launched. Otherwise he knew their certain retreat would throw his force into a state of confusion. The only way to prevent them from melting away to their farms was to march the whole lot back to the fort and make the most of them. Maybe their backs could be stiffened by the example of the regular troops. But even that was doubtful. A good many former Americans said they wanted to join Hull as soon as he crossed into Canada.

At last, on July 12, a bright and lovely Sunday, Hull resolved to make the crossing even though two hundred of his men continued to stand on their constitutional rights. He feared further mutinies if he kept his troops inactive. He imagined Canadian settlers would feel themselves liberated from the British yoke once he landed and that they and the Indians would stay out of the war. His landing was unopposed.

Sandwich was a pleasant little garden village, almost every house set in a small orchard where peaches, grapes, and apples flourished. The conquering general seized the most imposing residence, belonging to Lieutenant-Colonel

François Bâby. The Bâby family and the Hull family had been on intimate terms, but all Hull could say was that "circumstances are changed now."

Hull scarcely had landed when he insisted on issuing a proclamation intended to disperse the militia and frighten the inhabitants, many of whom were either terrified of his troops or secretly sympathetic to his cause. Most had fled. Those who remained welcomed the invaders as friends. They waved white handkerchiefs and flags from the windows and cried out, "We like the Americans." In spite of this, Hull couldn't resist issuing a bombastic proclamation that seemed designed to set the Canadians on edge.

". . . Separated by an immense ocean and an extensive Wilderness from Great Britain you have no participation in her counsels, no interest in her conduct," the proclamation said. "You have felt her Tyranny, you have seen her injustice, but I do not ask *you* to avenge the one or redress the other. . . . I tender you the valuable blessings of Civil, Political, & Religious Liberty. . . . In the name of my *Country* and by the authority of my Government I promise you protection . . . remain at your homes, Pursue your peaceful and customary avocations. Raise not your hands against your brethren. . . . You will be emancipated from tyranny and oppression and restored to the dignified status of free men."

"If the barbarous and Savage policy of Great Britain be pursued and the savages let loose to murder our Citizens and butcher our women and children, this war, will be a war of extermination . . . . No white man found fighting by the Side of an Indian will be taken prisoner. Instant destruction will be his Lot. . . . I doubt not your courage and firmness; I will not doubt your attachment to Liberty. If you tender your services voluntarily they will be accepted readily."

"The United States offers you *Peace, Liberty,* and *Security* your choice lies between these, & *War, Slavery,* and *Destruction,* Choose then, but choose wisely. . . ."

The General, who was afraid of the Indians, hoped that the document would force his opposite number at Fort Amherstburg to follow the lead of the United States and adopt a policy of native neutrality. At the very minimum it ought to frighten the settlers and the militia into refusing to bear arms. That was its immediate effect. The Canadian militia were terrified. Within three days the force of newly recruited soldiers was reduced by half as the farm boys deserted to their homes.

But Hull had overstated his case. These were farmers he was addressing, not revolutionaries. Colonial politics touched very few. They didn't feel like slaves. They already had enough peace, liberty, and security to satisfy them. This tax-free province was not America at the time of the Boston Tea Party. Why was Hull asking them to free themselves from tyranny? In the words of one, if they had been under real tyranny, "they could at any time have crossed the line to the United States."

Hull made another error. He threatened that anyone found fighting beside the Indians could expect no quarter.

That rankled. *Everybody* would be fighting with the Indians; it wouldn't be a matter of choice. Some of the militiamen who had secretly hoped to go over to Hull in the confusion of battle had a change of heart. What was the point of deserting if the Americans intended to kill them on capture?

Hull's sudden action didn't fit the Upper Canadian mood. It was a pioneer society, not a frontier society. No Daniel Boones stalked the Canadian forests, ready to knock off an Injun with a Kentucky rifle or do battle over an imagined slight. The Methodist circuit riders kept the people law-abiding and temperate; prosperity kept them content. The Sabbath was looked on with reverence; card playing and horse racing were considered sinful diversions; the demon rum had yet to become a problem. There was little theft, less violence. Simple pastimes tied to the land – barn raisings, corn huskings, threshing bees – served as an outlet for the spirited. The new settlers wouldn't volunteer to fight; but most were prepared, if forced, to bear arms for their new country and to march when ordered. Hull's proclamation and his subsequent actions had the opposite effect from the one he intended. It helped turn the newcomers into patriotic Canadians.

CHAPTER SEVEN
"Why does the army dally?"

SITTING IN SANDWICH that July, Hull's troops became restless. Ever since the day of the landing, they had expected that Hull would sweep down the river to attack the British fort at Amherstburg.

Why was the army dallying? That was a question that Robert Lucas, one of Hull's scouts, asked rhetorically in his diary. ". . . Had proper energy been used, we might have been in Malden [Amherstburg] now, we are tampering with them until they will be able to drive us back across the river."

As a scout, Lucas was used to acting on his own, swiftly and decisively, or with a small company of rangers. His job was to move silently ahead of the main force, protecting it from ambush and feeling out the lay of the land. Now he wanted to get on with it. Once Fort Amherstburg's guns were silenced, the way to Upper Canada lay wide open. The only other British forts on the Western frontier were at the other end of Lake Erie and along the Niagara River. A second American army had been sent to attack those strong points. Its task was to cause a diversion, to pin down the defending British, and to prevent reinforcements from reaching Fort Amherstburg.

Lucas was one of many who thought that speed was essential. Amherstburg must be attacked and taken before Brock could divert more men to its defence. As a scout, he was used to swift, flexible movements. In Hull's mixed bag of raw recruits, untrained civilians, professional commanders, and elected leaders, he was a real mixture – general, captain, and private soldier rolled into one. This sprang out of his country's awkward military philosophy, which disdained the idea of a standing army and relied on volunteers for the nation's defence. For some time Robert Lucas had been a brigadier-general in the Ohio state militia. Eager to serve in the regular army, he applied in April of 1812 for a captain's commission. But a few days later, before it came through, McArthur ordered him to transmit from his brigade a proportion of the twelve hundred men required from the state in the coming war. What was he to do? Thirsty for action, Lucas set an example to his men by enlisting as a private in a volunteer company. To add to the confusion, the men elected his younger brother, John, as their captain.

Now, at Sandwich, Lucas was disgusted. Why indeed did the army dally? Hull wasn't short of supplies. He had sent his best regimental commander, Colonel Duncan McArthur, USA to raid the farms, the barns and the fields up the Thames for food and equipment. McArthur, a former member of the

Ohio legislature, had been voted Colonel of the 1st Regiment of Ohio volunteers. It was said of him that he "looks more like a go-ahead soldier than any of his brother officers." But to a later English visitor, he was "dirty and butcher-like, very unlike a soldier in appearance, seeming half savage and dressed like a backwoodsman; generally considered being only fit for hard knocks and Indian warfare" – which, of course was exactly the kind of contest that was facing him.

McArthur lived up to his reputation. He and his men, moving without blankets and provisions, lived off the country and left a trail of devastation in their wake. They penetrated sixty miles (96 km) into the heart of Upper Canada: a land of stumps and snake fences; of cabins and shanties of basswood and cedar; of Dutch lofts and clay ovens; of grist mills, fanning mills and windmills; of chicken hutches, corn cribs, hog pens, and cattle sheds; of pickled pork and pigeon pie and fresh milk kept cool in underground sheds; of oxen hitched in tandem, furrowing the glistening fields, and raw-boned men in homespun linsey-woolsey scything the tawny harvest of midsummer.

John McGregor, a trader and merchant, was one who lost everything. He had removed his goods to a neighbour's house on the Thames for safety – flour, merchandise, grain, livestock. He lost them all and almost lost his life as well, fleeing in haste when he learned that McArthur intended to shoot him on sight in the belief that he and his neighbour were rousing the Indians and the militia to resistance.

Farmers and townspeople were beggared by the raiders. Jean-Baptiste Beniteau's orchard of sixty fruit trees was destroyed, his fences and pickets reduced to ashes. His neighbour, Jean-Baptiste Ginac, was looted of all his livestock, pork, flour, oats and corn. Another Jean-Baptiste, surnamed Fourneau, lost 480 bushels (175 hectolitres) of grain, all his cider, furniture, and his winter supplies of wood. A fourth, Jean-Baptiste Boismier, saw his entire fortune of 620 skins, together with his livestock, tools, utensils, and harvested corn go to the enemy.

The raiding party returned in five days with two hundred barrels of flour, four hundred blankets, and wagons loaded with whiskey, salt, cloth, guns, ammunition, household goods, tools – even boats. They destroyed green fields, ransacked homes, levelled orchards, trampled corn, and burned fences – actions that enraged the settlers and helped to turn them against their former comrades.

Hull's men made no allowance for old comrades. Lieutenant-Colonel François Bâby, whose house had become Hull's headquarters, had tried to save some of his chattels by hauling them off to a friend's home three miles (five km) away. But Hull dispatched a party of dragoons with six wagons who took everything at gun point and then, emboldened, sliced up one of Bâby's finest coats with their sabres. Bâby's loss was staggering. He reckoned it at 2,678 pounds sterling.

Besieged by complaints, McArthur brushed them all aside and promised that everything would be paid for. Hull, he explained, had such footing in Canada that the British would never be able to drive him out. It certainly looked that way. At Fort Amherstburg the situation was deteriorating. Militia service was working a real hardship on those Canadian families who depended upon the able-bodied for their livelihood. Hundreds deserted. Those who remained loyal had no one to harvest their wheat and so lost it all to rot. St. George, the commander, was forced to release the oldest and least efficient to return to their farms. Others began to slip away. On July 8 he had 850 militia under his command; a week later the number had dropped to 471.

Meanwhile, Robert Lucas, who had seen more fighting than most of his followers in Hull's army, was back in action. On July 16, when Hull ordered two of his regimental commanders to search out the enemy country as far as the River Aux Canards, three miles (five km) north of Amherstburg, Lucas offered to go along. The war would make his reputation, and he eventually rose to become governor of Ohio.

Once again, Lucas and the rangers were out in front of the main body. Colonel Lewis Cass of the 2nd Regiment, Ohio Volunteers, took charge. In spite of his lack of training, he outranked his fellow commander, Lieutenant-Colonel James Miller, a regular officer in command of the 4th Infantry Division. Cass was eager for glory and action. A stocky, coarse-featured lawyer of flaming ambition, he was U.S. Marshal for his state. Unlike Miller, a disciplined career officer, he didn't hesitate to bad-mouth Hull in public.

Cass decided to ford the river upstream and circle round

the enemy, while Miller pinned down the sentries at the bridge which was held by a small detachment of British regulars and Menomenee Indians.

Faced with an attack on their rear, the British retired. Cass couldn't pursue the chase because a stream blocked the way. But the British sentries on the bridge, John Dean and James Hancock, held their ground and became the first soldiers to shed their blood on Canadian soil.

And here, the Americans came up against the stubborn fighting qualities of the British regulars. Dean, with an arm broken by a musket ball, fought on with his bayonet until he was knocked to the ground and disarmed. Hancock, bleeding from at least two wounds and unable to support himself, continued to fight on his knees until he was captured. He died that night and was scalped by one of the Indians who sold the trophy to the British.

Now the Americans held the bridge – the bridge that could lead the army to Amherstburg. Cass and Miller both thought the entire force should move to within striking distance of the fort. But Hull dithered. He would not start an attack until his heavy artillery was ready. The fort could have been taken by an infantry assault, but Hull was convinced the slaughter would be appalling and so the bridge was abandoned.

Hull had other concerns. He did not know quite what was happening on the rest of the Niagara frontier. It was essential that an American army be in place along that river. Otherwise there was nothing to stop the British from concentrating their entire armies against him. He had been promised there would be diversions on the Niagara to support his invasion, but the communications were so bad that the General had no way of knowing whether that had been done.

Meanwhile he was tormented by another problem. He was certain that Colonel Cass was trying to pressure him for reasons of personal ambition. He felt his authority slipping away. His officers' complaints were beginning to destroy his influence. He called council after council to quell their impatience, but it only eroded his command.

He was determined not to advance until he was absolutely certain of success. But how long would it take to prepare the cannon? Two days? Two weeks? After each meeting the time stretched. Hull feared defeat. Defeat would mean starvation for the troops and worse devastation by the Indians. The militia feared the Indians. And Dickson's Menomenee, and Tecumseh's followers were terrifying the raw recruits, who on one occasion said "they would rather be killed by their own officers" who were trying to keep them in line "than by the damned Indians."

There was savagery on both sides. The first Indian scalp was taken during one skirmish by Captain William McCullough of the Rangers, who described in a letter to his wife how he tore it from the corpse's head with his teeth. William Beall and his fellow prisoners at Amherstburg heard of these skirmishes and hoped for his speedy deliverance. Hull's army was camped within reach. But instead of seeing American soldiers marching into town he was greeted by a more macabre spectacle.

Thomas McKee of the Canadian Indian Department arrived at the head of about fifty Indians, all naked except for their breech cloths. McKee, also dressed as a native, halted opposite the gaping prisoners and hoisted a fresh scalp fastened to a long pole, which he shook exultantly, all the time taunting the captives with savage cries. It would, Beall wrote, "have chilled the blood of a Laplander . . . crimsoned the tawny cheek of an unrelenting Turk." Actually, the scalp was that of the unfortunate British sentry, Hancock – McKee's British ally.

Beall and his fellow prisoners couldn't understand what was keeping Hull from attacking. The optimism, good humour, and gallantry of those first days in captivity were gone. Beall no longer saw the British as gentlemen but as monsters. He was now totally disillusioned with Hull. The British officers and soldiers were laughing at the American general, and as Beall wrote, "he is now the object of their jest and ridicule instead of being as he was formerly, their terror and greatest fear."

On July 26 Hull was shaken by an alarming piece of intelligence. A ship flying British colours was brought about by a shot from the shore. Aboard was a group of American citizens and soldiers led by Lieutenant Porter Hanks, the former commander at Michilimackinac who had been paroled. Now for the first time Hull learned of Mackinac's fall – a major disaster. Hull was convinced that "the northern hives of Indians" would shortly come "swarming down in every direction."

He felt himself surrounded by Indians. He figured there were perhaps two or three thousand advancing from Mackinac, not to mention the Iroquois of the Grand Valley who, though still neutral, might still join the British at any time. And in front of them at Amherstburg lay another potent force – hundreds more Indians led by the great Tecumseh. Hull feared those more than he did the handful of British regulars.

By the end of July William Beall and the others had lost all hope of rescue from the fort. "I can hardly think that Genl. H. will be defeated," Beall wrote, "but appearances justify such a belief. I am confident that he will not take Malden though three hundred men could do it."

CHAPTER EIGHT
General Hull backs down

HULL KNEW THAT HE had to contact the wagon train of supplies, which he desperately needed to feed his army. To do that he sent an armed body of 200 Ohio volunteers across the Detroit River to intercept the wagons before they could be captured by the British. The cattle and pack animals were moving on to the River Raisin after a gruelling trek through dense thickets and treacherous mire. Now, unable to continue on to Detroit under the guns of Fort Amherstburg, they were stalled.

As usual, Robert Lucas was out ahead of the relief party. He and two fellow rangers lay in the bushes, watched by unseen eyes. Beside him was the ranger captain, McCullough – the same man who had the dubious distinction of the being the only American thus far to take an Indian scalp. At first light McCullough and his scouts rose, mounted their horses, and made a wide sweep around the detachment. They scented trouble, noting tracks on the road and trails in the grass – evidence that a party of Indians had been watching them during the night. Out on the river, a faint *splish-splash* penetrated the shroud of mist that hung out over the water. Oars! The British were intent on capturing the supply line.

McCullough, Lucas and the others rode on through the Wyandot village of Maguaga – deserted now, the houses empty. News of the victory at Michilimackinac had tipped the scales, and the Wyandot tribe wanted to be on the winning side.

The road forked around a cornfield. Lucas and a companion took the right fork; McCullough took the left and rode into an ambush. Lucas heard a volley of shots but before he could reach him, the scalper was himself scalped, tomahawked, riddled with musket balls. The rear guard was in a panic, but the Indians had already vanished into the tall corn.

Shaken, the detachment moved on, leaving three corpses under a cover of bark and ignoring a Frenchman's warning that a large force of Indians was waiting for them at Brownstown. The Americans didn't trust the French settlers, some of whom were pro-British and tried to confuse them with false reports.

The war party moved in double file. Between the files mounted men escorted the mail – a packet of personal letters written by Hull's soldiers to their families and friends, many of them critical of their general. More significantly, the mail contained Hull's dispatches to Washington, revealing both his plans and his pessimism.

Brownstown village lay ahead, but Brownstown Creek first had to be crossed. The only practical ford lay in a narrow opening with thick bushes on the right and fields of tall corn on the opposite bank and on the left – a perfect spot for an ambush. Lucas, the old hand, recognized the danger and rode along the right column warning the men to see that their muskets were freshly primed.

Tecumseh had recognized it too. He and his followers lay flat on their bellies directly ahead. As the Shawnee leader silently waited, the American files closed up to cross the creek. Then, at a range of no more than twenty-five yards (twenty-three m), the Indians rose out of the corn, their high-pitched war cries mingling with the explosion of their weapons.

Lucas's horse was shot and toppled sideways against another wounded animal, pitching its rider onto the ground, his musket flying from his hand. Weaponless, Lucas tried with little success to rally his men. The odds were twenty to one in favour of the Americans, but the Indians were shouting so wildly that they believed themselves outnumbered.

It was not necessary to order a retreat – the Americans flung down their weapons, scattered the mail, and plunged headlong back the way they came, actually outrunning their pursuers who followed them for three miles (five km) before giving up the chase. Lucas, covering their retreat as best he could, was the last man to escape.

The Battle of Brownstown, as it came to be called, represented a setback for Hull. The detachment had lost eighteen men killed and twenty wounded. Some seventy were missing, many hiding in the bushes. The following day most straggled back. Worse than the loss of seven officers was the abandoning of the mail. That raised Brock's spirits because here, in letters home, was strong evidence of the discontent and illness in the American ranks and of the lack of confidence in the leadership.

Even more important was Hull's letter of August 4 to the American Secretary of War outlining the critical situation of his army, pleading for another two thousand men, and expressing his deep-seated fear of the Indians, who he believed would shortly be swarming down through Mackinac Island.

At Brownstown, meanwhile, a strong detachment of the British 41st – John Richardson's regiment – accompanied by militia and civilian volunteers had crossed the river. Too late to take part in the skirmish, they were prepared to frustrate any further attempt by Hull to open the supply lines. The British waited all night, unable to light a fire, shivering in the damp without blankets or provisions.

Now they were exposed to a spectacle calculated to make them shudder further. The Indians held a young American captive and were intent on killing him. Major Adam Muir, who headed the expedition, did his best to intervene. He even offered a barrel of rum and articles of clothing if the prisoner's life was spared. But then a series of piercing cries issued from the forest – the funeral convoy of a young chief, Blue Jacket, the only casualty among Tecumseh's followers. Four tribesmen carried in the body. Thomas Verchères de

Boucherville, a citizen volunteer and experienced fur trader from Amherstburg, realized there was no hope for the American because the Indians were intent on avenging their chief, who placed the corpse at the captive's feet.

The oldest Potawatomi chief raised his hatchet over the prisoner as a group of Indian women drew near. At the chief's signal, one plunged a butcher knife into the victim's head, a second stabbed him in the side, and the chief dispatched him with a tomahawk. Tecumseh, who would certainly have prevented the execution – for he did not believe in this kind of savagery – was not present.

Young de Boucherville would never shake the incident from his memory. "We all stood around overcome by an acute sense of shame," he wrote later. "We felt implicated in some way in this murder . . . and yet, under the circumstances what could we do? The life of that man undoubtedly belonged to the inhuman chief. The government had desperate need of these Indian allies. Our garrison was weak and these warriors were numerous enough to impose their will upon us. If we were to rebuke them in this crisis . . . they would withdraw from the conflict, and retire to their own country on the Missouri whence they had come to join us." De Boucherville was coming to realize what others would soon grasp, that the British were as much prisoners of the Indians as the young American whose tomahawked corpse lay stretched out before them.

Meanwhile in his headquarters in François Bâby's unfinished mansion in Sandwich, Hull continued to waver. He had promised his impatient officers that he would attack the fort whether the artillery was ready or not, but now he had second thoughts. The British controlled the river. He could not float his artillery downriver in the teeth of their gunboats. But his enemies could cross the river at will and could harass the supply lines. He considered a retreat but backed off after a stormy meeting with Colonel McArthur. He brooded, changed his mind, called a council of his commanders, and finally agreed to adopt their plan of attacking the fort. He would move against it at the head of his troops "and in whatever manner the affair may terminate, it will never reflect on you, gentlemen."

At this dazzling news, Robert Lucas, back from the humiliation at Brownstown, was exultant. A wave of good cheer surged over the camp. Even the sick rose from their beds to seize their muskets. Orders were issued for five days' rations, and ammunition and whiskey was loaded onto the wagons. All necessary tents, baggage and boats were to be sent back to Detroit.

Then, on the afternoon of August 7, hard on the heels of news from Brownstown, came an express rider with dispatches for Hull from two American commanders on the Niagara Frontier. Boats loaded with British troops had been seen crossing Lake Erie and headed for Amherstburg. More British regulars accompanied by Canadian militia and Indians were enroute from Niagara by boat to the fort. Since the British controlled the lakes there was nothing the Americans could do to stop them.

At this point, both opposing generals were totally in the dark. Each believed his own position to be doubtful and his adversary's superior. Brock had decided on a risky move – to *Brit* reduce his forces on the Niagara frontier to a minimum in order to bolster the defence of Amherstburg. Certainly he expected Hull to attack his weak garrison at any moment. He was desperate to reinforce it but despaired of holding it against great numbers.

But Hull was badly rattled. Isolated on Canadian soil and faced with alarming reports of more British soldiers arriving, he was convinced that Brock's combined force was not only stronger than his own, but growing at an alarming rate. Hull, unlike Brock, was no gambler. He felt doomed by bad luck – the supposedly friendly Indians turning against him, the blocking of his supply train, and now a fresh onslaught of fighting men. The general saw himself and his troops suddenly trapped in an unfriendly country, their backs to the river, their food running out, surrounded by Indians, facing Brock's regulars and Tecumseh's braves. Hull was convinced he must get his army back to American soil, with the barrier of the Detroit River between him and his enemies.

He broke the news to his officers. At that, the swarthy McArthur refused to give any further opinions as to the movement of the army. Hull suggested hesitantly that the army might withdraw as far the Maumee. Cass told him that if he did that every man in the Ohio militia would leave him. That put an end to that. The army would withdraw to Detroit but no farther.

VSA Lewis Cass was infuriated. To him, Hull's decision was fatal and unaccountable. This final about face, he was convinced, had dispirited the troops and destroyed the last vestige of confidence they had in their commander.

He was undoubtedly right. It would have been far better if Hull had never crossed the river in the first place, at least until the supply lines were secure.

A sense of astonishment mingled with a feeling of disgrace rippled through the camp. Robert Lucas was one who felt it. The orders to recross the river under cover of darkness were, he thought, especially dastardly. But cross the army must, and when night fell the men slunk into their boats. By the following morning there was scarcely an American soldier left on Canadian soil.

CHAPTER NINE
Brock takes the offensive

Brit

ISAAC BROCK WAS having trouble with his legislature in Little York. He was convinced that the legislators, expecting an American victory, were afraid to take any action that might displease the conquerors. The majority of Canadians, who had no say in their own government, were obviously unwilling to fight. But Brock was determined to rally them by harsh methods if need be. He wanted to suspend civil rights and establish martial law, but the legislature would not go along with him. Pinned down at York by his civilian duties, he took what action he could to stiffen the defence at Fort Amherstburg by sending a younger and more efficient officer, Lieutenant-Colonel Henry Procter, to take over from the confused and harassed St. George.

Brock realized Amherstburg was vital. If Hull seized it – as he seemed likely to do – he could sweep up the Thames or turn eastward to attack the British rear at Fort George on the Niagara and link up with the second American army already forming along that gorge. Brock did not yet know that Hull had retreated across the river.

But Brock was weary of idle chatter in the legislature. He dismissed that body August 5 and, with the consent of his appointed council, declared martial law anyway. He decided on a mighty gamble. He would gather what troops he could, speed post-haste to Amherstburg at their head, and, if that fort had not fallen, provoke Hull into a fight and then try to move on to the Niagara frontier before the Americans attacked.

He was taking a long chance, but he had little choice. Off he went, moving swiftly southwest through the province calling for volunteers to accompany him to Amherstburg. Five hundred rushed to apply, many the sons of British veterans. He could only take half that number. But the York Volunteers became Brock's favourite militia unit, including among its officers some of the finest names of the Upper Canada aristocracy. The war would entrench them into a tight little governing body soon to be known as "The Family Compact", so called because so many members of this élite group were related by blood or marriage.

Brock reached port at Dover on the north shore of Lake Erie on August 8. There, he hoped enough boats had been commandeered to move his entire force to Amherstburg. But at Dover, Brock found that not nearly enough boats had been provided, and most of those available were leaky, uncaulked, and dilapidated. It required a day to make ten of them ready, and these were in such bad shape that the men grew exhausted from constant bailing.

The flotilla could move no faster than the slowest vessel,

the hundred-ton (ninety tonnes) schooner *Nancy*, which had to be man-handled over the narrow neck of the Long Point Peninsula – a back-breaking task that required the energy of all the boat crews.

The troops were held up by a thunderstorm but remained in good spirits. Brock wrote that, "in no instance have I witnessed greater cheerfulness and constancy than were displayed by these Troops under the fatigue of a long journey in Boats and during extremely bad Weather." In Brock's words, "their conduct throughout excited my admiration."

That admiration was mutual. At one point Brock's own boat struck a sunken rock. His boat crew went to work with oars and poles. When they failed to push her free, the General, in full uniform, leapt over the side, waist deep in water. In an instant, the others followed and soon had the boat floating. Brock climbed back aboard, opened his liquor case, and gave every man a glass of spirits. The news of that act, spreading from boat to boat, animated the force.

The weather again turned capricious on August 11. The wind dropped. The men, wet and exhausted from lack of sleep, were forced to row in relays for hours. Then, a sudden squall forced the flotilla once more into the shore. That night the weather cleared, and the impatient general made another attempt to get under way, this time in the dark, his boat leading with a lantern in the stern.

They sailed all night, the boats too crowded for the men to lie down. The following morning they learned that Hull had retreated across the river to Detroit. At Point Pelee that afternoon, some of the men boiled their pork while others dropped exhausted onto the beach. Early next morning they set off again, and at eight in the forenoon, they straggled into Amherstburg, exhausted from rowing, their faces peeling from sunburn.

Brock was there before them. Unable to rest, the general and a vanguard of troops had left the previous afternoon and reached their objective shortly before midnight on August 13. Lieutenant-Colonel Procter and Matthew Elliott of the Indian department were waiting on the quayside. Across the water came the rattle of musketry, which startled Brock. Elliott explained that Indians camped on Bois Blanc Island were expressing their joy at the arrival of reinforcements. Brock told them not to waste their ammunition. Midnight had passed by, but he could not sleep. First, he had to read the dispatches and mail captured at Brownstown. He sat in Elliott's study with his aide, Major J.B. Glegg, the yellow light from tallow candles, flickering across the desk, strewn with maps and papers.

Suddenly the door opened, and Elliott stood before him accompanied by a tall Indian, dressed in a plain suit of tanned deer skin, fringed at the seams, and wearing leather moccasins heavily ornamented with porcupine quills. This was clearly a leader of stature. In his nose he wore three silver ornaments in the shape of coronets, and from his neck was hung, on a string of coloured wampum, a large silver medallion of George III.

The Indian was beaming. Glegg got an instant impression of energy and decision. This must be Tecumseh.

Brock rose, hand outstretched. The contrast was striking: the British general – fair, large-limbed, blue-eyed, impeccable in his scarlet jacket, blue and white riding trousers, and Hessian boots – towered over the lithe figure of the Shawnee. Brief salutations followed. Brock explained about the waste of ammunition. Tecumseh agreed. Each man had taken the other's measure and both were impressed. According to Brock, "A more sagacious and gallant Warrior does not I believe exist. He was the admiration of everyone who conversed with him." Tecumseh's comment, delivered to his followers, was blunter. "This," he said, "is a *man*!"

Brock called a council of his officers and asked for a military assessment. Tecumseh urged an immediate attack on Detroit and unrolled a strip of elm bark. Then he pulled his scalping knife from his belt and proceed to scratch out an accurate map of the fort and its surroundings.

It was clear the British and the Indians would be outnumbered. When Brock polled his officers, all but one advised against trying to cross the river.

Brock listened carefully to his subordinates' reservations and then spoke. Nothing, he said, could be gained by delay. "I have decided on crossing, and now, gentlemen, instead of any further advice, I entreat of you to give me your cordial and hearty support."

The following morning, standing beneath a great oak on the outskirts of the fort, he addressed several hundred

Indians representing a dozen tribes on both sides of the border. He had come, said Brock, to battle the Long Knives who had invaded the country of the King, their father. The Long Knives were trying to force the British and Indians from their lands. If the Indians would make common cause with the British, the combined forces would soon drive the enemy back to the boundaries of Indian territory.

Tecumseh rose to reply. The hazel eyes flashed, and the oval face darkened as he conjured up the memory of the Battle of Tippecanoe:

"They suddenly came against us with a great force while I was absent, and destroyed our village and slew our warriors."

All the bitterness against the land hunger of the frontier settlements was revived:

"They came to us hungry and cut off the hands of our brothers who gave them corn. We gave them rivers of fish and they poisoned our fountains. We gave them forest-clad mountains and valleys full of game, and in return what did they give our warriors and women? Rum and trinkets and a grave!"

Brock had no intention of revealing the details of his attack plan to such a large assembly. But when the meeting was finished he invited Tecumseh and a few older chiefs to meet him at Elliott's house. There, through interpreters, he explained his strategy. But he was concerned about alcohol. Could Tecumseh prevent his followers from drinking to excess? The Shawnee replied that his people had promised to abstain from all spirits until they had humbled the Long Knives. Brock had one further act of diplomacy. He issued a general order intending to heal the wounds caused by Hull's divisive proclamation – the one that threatened to "exterminate" anyone who fought beside the Indians. He was willing to believe, he said, that the conduct of the deserters proceeded "from an anxiety to get in their harvest and not from any predilection for the principles or government of the United States." That statement helped to unite the people behind him. Hull had deserted them. Brock, by implication, promised an amnesty. As he rode the same afternoon past the ripening apple trees to Sandwich, he knew he was passing through friendly country.

CHAPTER TEN
Brock's ultimatum

MEANWHILE, IN DETROIT, all was not well with Hull's army. Colonel Lewis Cass was seething with frustration over what he felt were the failures of his commander. From the outset he had thought of Hull as a weak, old man. Now, other more sinister possibilities began to form in his mind. Cass was contemplating something very close to treason, a word he would shortly apply to his commanding officer.

His disillusionment with Hull was shared by his fellow officers and soon filtered down through the ranks. As the scout, Robert Lucas, wrote to a friend: "Never was there a more Patriotic army . . . neither was there ever an army that had it more completely in their power to accomplish every object of their Desire than the Present, And must now be sunk into Disgrace for want of a General at their head. . . ."

The army was close to mutiny. A petition was circulating among the troops urging that Hull be replaced by McArthur. The three militia generals, Cass, McArthur, and James Findlay, met with Miller and offered to depose Hull

if he would take command. But Miller refused, being a regular soldier. McArthur also refused, and all three turned to Cass, who agreed to write secretly to Governor Meigs of Ohio, urging him to march at once with two thousand men. Meigs, it was assumed, would depose Hull. Cass wrote, "that this army has been reduced to a critical and alarming situation." He added, "believe all the bearer will tell you. Believe it, however it may astonish you; as much as if told by one of us." He did not care to put anything more detailed into writing.

By this time Hull knew of the incipient plot against him, but hesitated to arrest the ringleaders, fearing perhaps a general uprising. However, he had a perfect excuse for ridding himself temporarily of the leading malcontents. Captain Henry Brush at the head of the supply train, still pinned down at the River Raisin, had discovered a backdoor route to Detroit. It was twice as long as the river road, but hidden from Fort Amherstburg. When he asked for an escort, Hull was only too pleased to dispatch both Cass and McArthur with 350 men for that task. They would leave Detroit at noon on August 14.

Of course, the general was weakening his own garrison, in spite of the strong evidence that the British were now at Sandwich, directly across the river, planning an attack. What was in Hull's mind? Had he already given up? He had in his possession a letter, intercepted from a British courier, written by Lieutenant-Colonel Procter to Captain Roberts at Michilimackinac, informing him that the British force facing Detroit was so strong that he needs send no more than five thousand Indians to support it!

That was a sobering revelation. Brock and Tecumseh faced Hull across the river, but now at his rear he saw another horde of painted savages. He could not know the letter was a fake, purposely planted by Brock and Procter, who already had an insight into Hull's troubled state of mind through the captured documents. Actually, there were only a few hundred Indians at Mackinac, and on August 12 they were in no condition to go anywhere, being "as drunk as Ten Thousand Devils" in the words of one observer. Brock knew well that the threat of the Indians was just as valuable as their presence and a good deal less expensive.

Brock was also completing the secret construction of a battery directly across from Detroit – one long eighteen-pound (eight kg) gun, two long twelve-pounders (five kg), and a couple of mortars – hidden for the moment behind a building in a screen of oak.

Lieutenant James Dalliba, Hull's gunnery officer, who had his own guns in the centre of Fort Detroit, asked Hull if he might open fire. "Sir, if you will give me permission, I will clear the enemy on the opposite shore from the lower batteries."

Dalliba would not soon forget Hull's reply.

"Mr. Dalliba, I will make an agreement with the enemy that if they will never fire on me, I will never fire on them," and off he rode, remarking that, "Those who live in glass houses must take care how they throw stones."

The following morning, to the army's astonishment, Hull had a large marquee, striped red and blue, pitched in the centre of camp, just south of the walls of the fort. Many in his army believed that Hull was in league with the British and the coloured tent was intended as a signal.

In a barrack room, a court of inquiry under Lieutenant-Colonel Miller was investigating Porter Hanks's surrender of Mackinac. Hanks had asked for the hearing to clear his name. But part way through the testimony, an officer looking out onto the river spotted a boat crossing from the opposite side under a white flag. Miller adjourned the hearing which would never be reopened.

Up the bank came Brock's two aides, Major Glegg and Lieutenant-Colonel John Macdonell, with a message for Hull. They were blindfolded and confined to a house in the town near the fort while Hull pondered Brock's ultimatum.

"The force at my disposal authorizes me to require of you the immediate surrender of Fort Detroit. . . ."

The force at his disposal! Brock had, at the very most, thirteen hundred men; Hull had more than two thousand. Here was Brock proposing to attack a fortified position with an inferior force – an adventure that Hull, in giving up Amherstburg, had said would require odds of two-to-one.

But Brock had studied his man and knew his vulnerable spot. He wrote: "It is far from my intention to join in a war of extermination; but you must be aware that the numerous body of Indians who have attached themselves to my troops will be beyond my control the moment the contest commences. . . ."

What Brock was threatening, of course, was a war of extermination – a bloody battle in which, if necessary, he was quite prepared to accept the slaughter of prisoners and of innocent civilians, including women and children. He was, in short, contemplating total war more than a century before that phrase came into common use. The war was starting to escalate, as all wars must. As impatience for victory clouded compassion, the end began to justify the means.

Like other commanders, Brock soothed his conscience with the excuse that he couldn't control his native allies. Nonetheless, he was quite eager to use them. The conflict, which began so softly and civilly, was beginning to brutalize both sides. The same men who censured the Indians for dismembering non-combatants with tomahawks were quite prepared to blow the limbs off soldiers and civilians alike with twenty-four pound cannon balls. Though it might offer some comfort to the attacker, the range of the weapons made little difference to the victim.

Hull mulled over Brock's extraordinary document for more than three hours. At last, he wrote: "I have no other reply, than to inform you, that I am prepared to meet any force which may be at your disposal, and any consequences which may result from any exertion that you may think proper to make."

Now the village of Detroit was alive with people running

toward the fort carrying their family possessions or bearing their valuables. Across the river British troops were chopping down oaks and removing the buildings that masked the cannon. Hull immediately sent a messenger to recall the party under Cass and McArthur, who had become entangled in a swamp some twenty-five miles (forty km) away. The troops in Detroit, knowing their force to be superior, were astonished at what they considered the insolence of the British.

As soon as Brock's aides were safely across the river with a message for their general, the British cannonade commenced. Hundreds of kilogrammes of cast iron hurtled across the wide river, tearing into walls and trees and plunging through rooftops, but doing little damage. James Dalliba, with his battery of seven twenty-four pound cannon, replied immediately to the first British volley. He stood on the ramparts until he saw the smoke and flash of the British cannon, then shouted, "Down!", allowing his men to drop behind the parapet before the shot struck. The British were aiming directly at his battery, attempting to put it out of action.

A large pear tree was blocking the guns and giving the British an aiming point. A young militia volunteer, John Miller, started to cut it down. As he was hacking away, a cannon ball finished the job for him. Miller turned and shouted across the water: "Send us another, John Bull; you can cut faster than I can!"

The artillery duel continued until well after dark. The

people scrambled after every burst, ducking behind doors, clinging to walls until they became used to the flash and roar. A mortar shell, its fuse burning brightly, fell into a house on Woodward Avenue. It tore its way through the roof, continued to the upper storey and into the dining room, around which the family were sitting. It ripped through the table, continued through the floor and into the cellar as the owners dashed for safety. They were no sooner clear than the shell exploded with such power that it tore the roof away.

Hull's brigade major, Thomas Jesup, reported that two British warships were anchored in midstream just opposite Spring Wells, two miles (3.2 km) from the fort. The British, he said, appeared to be collecting boats for an invasion. Hull sent an aide to report on these movements and was told that the British vessel, *Queen Charlotte*, was anchored in the river but could be dislodged by one of the fort's twenty-four pounders. But Hull shook his head and found reasons why the gun couldn't be moved. To Jesup the commander seemed pale and much confused.

At ten that evening the cannonade ceased. Quiet descended upon the American camp. The night was clear, the sky tinselled with stars, the river glittering in the moonlight. At eleven, General Hull, fully clothed, his boots still laced, slumped down in the barrack square and tried to sleep. Even as he slumbered, Tecumseh and his Indians were slipping into their canoes and silently crossing to the American side.

CHAPTER ELEVEN
Surrender

THE BRITISH CROSSING began at dawn on August 16. Brock's couriers had scoured the countryside and roused the militia from the farms, emptying the mills and harvest fields. Now these raw troops gathered on the shore at McKee's Point, four hundred strong, waiting their turn to enter the boats and cross to the enemy's side. Brock again intended to deceive Hull into believing that his army was outnumbered by British regulars. To that end, he ordered that three hundred civilians cover their homespun with the cast-off crimson tunics of the 41st. It was one of several deceptions that the ingenious general had devised.

The Indians were already across, lurking in the forest, ready to attack Hull's flank and rear, should he resist the crossing.

The previous night they had executed their war dance – six hundred figures, leaping in the fire light, naked except for their breech cloths, some daubed in vermilion, others in blue clay, and still others tattooed with black and white from head to foot. But on this calm and beautiful Sunday

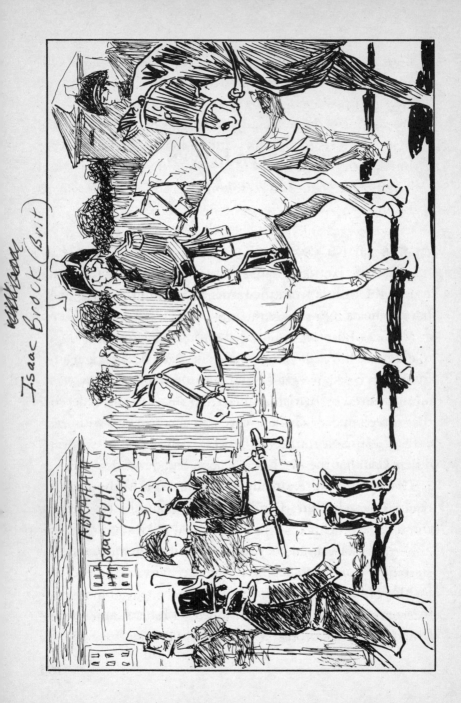

Isaac Brock (Brit)

ABRAHAM
Isaac Hull
(USA)

morning, a different spectacle presented itself. A soft, August sun was just rising as the troops climbed into the boats and pushed out into the river, their crimson jackets almost perfectly reflected in the glassy waters. Behind them, the green meadows and ripening orchards were tinted with the dawn light. Ahead, in the lead boat, stood the glittering figure of their general. Already cannon balls and mortar bombs were screaming overhead.

On the far bank, pocked and riven by springs (hence the name Spring Wells), the figure of Tecumseh could be discerned, astride a white mustang, surrounded by his chiefs. The enemy was not in sight, and the troops landed without incident or opposition.

Brock's plan was to outwit Hull, to draw him out of his fort, and do battle out in the open, where he believed his regulars could devastate the wavering American volunteers. Now, however, an Indian scout rode up with the word that enemy horsemen had been spotted three miles to the rear. That was the detachment, three hundred and fifty strong, that Hull had sent to the River Raisin and had recalled to reinforce Detroit. Suddenly Brock's position became precarious. His men were caught between the strong fortification and an advancing column in their rear. Without hesitation, the general changed his plans and decided on an immediate attack.

He drew up his troops in column and engaged in another deception. By doubling the distance between the sections he made his small force seem larger. His route to Detroit hugged the river bank on his right, protected by the guns of the ships in the river and by the battery at Sandwich. On his left, slipping through the cornfields and woods, were Tecumseh's Indians.

At the town gate, the forward troops could spot two long guns, positioned so they could cover the road. A single round shot, properly placed, was capable of knocking down a file of twenty-five men like dominoes. American gunners stood behind their weapons, with matches burning.

Brock, at the head of the line, rode impassively forward, a brilliant target in his cocked hat and gold epaulettes. An old friend, Colonel Robert Nichol, trotted up to remonstrate with his commander; "Pardon me, general, but I cannot forbear entreating you not to expose yourself thus. If we lose you, we lose all; let me, pray you, to allow the troops to pass on, led by their own officers."

To which Brock replied; "Master Nichol, I duly appreciate the advice you give me, but I feel that in addition to their sense of loyalty and duty, many here follow me from a feeling of personal regard, and I will never ask them to go where I do not lead them."

But why had the Americans' gun not fired? After the fact, there was a host of explanations. One was that Hull refused to give the order for reasons of cowardice or treason. Another, more plausible, was that the British were still out of effective range, and the American artillery commander was waiting until they drew closer so that his grapeshot could slow down the columns.

If that was his plan, Brock outwitted him. Suddenly the British column wheeled to the left through an orchard and into a ravine where they were protected from the enemy guns. Fifteen-year-old John Richardson, marching with the 41st, breathed more easily. Brock commandeered a farmhouse as his headquarters and climbed up the bank to reconnoitre his position.

The town of Detroit, a huddle of some three hundred houses lay before him. Its population, three-quarters French-speaking, was accustomed to siege and plunder, having been transferred three times by treaty, twice besieged by Indians, and burned to the ground only a few years previously. It was enclosed on three sides by a wooden stockade of fourteen foot (four m) pickets. Entrance could be gained only by three massive gates.

On the high ground to the northeast, covering three acres (1.2 hectares), sprawled the fort. It was built originally by the British and repaired by the Americans. It had an eleven foot (3.5 m) high earthen parapet, twelve feet thick (3.6 m). A ditch, six feet deep and twelve feet across (2 m x 3.6 m), together with a double row of pickets, each twice the height of a man, surrounded the whole. It was heavily armed with long guns, howitzers, and mortars. Most of the troops were quartered outside these walls.

The American position seemed impregnable but Brock had a secret weapon – psychology. Hull had already been led to believe that three hundred militiamen were regular troops. Now Tecumseh and his Indians were ordered to march in single file across an open space, out of range, but in full view of the fort. The spectacle had some of the quality of a vaudeville act. The Indians loped across the meadow, vanished into the forest, circled back and repeated the manoeuvre three times.

Hull's officers, who couldn't tell one Indian from another, thought they counted fifteen hundred painted savages, screeching and waving tomahawks. And so Hull was convinced he was outnumbered. Brock was still looking over his objective by himself some fifty yards (45 m) in front of his own troops when he spotted an American officer waving a white flag. The officer bore a note from his general. It appeared that Hull was on the verge of giving up without a fight.

In fact, at his post inside the palisade, William Hull appeared on the edge of nervous collapse. He had lost three of his battalion commanders. Cass and McArthur had not yet returned and Miller was too ill to stand up. A dozen Michigan volunteers on picket duty at the rear of the fort had allowed themselves to be captured by Tecumseh's Indians. Brush, in charge of the Michigan militia, believed that if an attack came his men would flee. The fort itself was jammed with soldiers, civilians, and cattle, all seeking refuge from the bombardment. It was difficult to manoeuvre.

The cannonade had unnerved Hull. He had seen plenty of blood in his revolutionary days, but now he was transfixed by a spectacle so horrifying it reduced him to jelly. Lieutenant Porter Hanks, relieved for the moment of appearing at his court of inquiry, had come in to the fort to visit an old friend and was standing in the doorway of the officers' mess with several others, when a sixteen-pound cannon ball came bouncing over the parapet and skipped across the open space. It struck Hanks in the midriff, cutting him in two, tore both legs off a second man, instantly killing him and mangling a third. A second cannon ball dispatched two more soldiers. Blood and brains spattered the walls and the gowns of some women who had sought refuge nearby. One fainted and the other began to scream.

Hull couldn't be sure from the distance who was dead, but a frightful thought crossed his mind: could it be his own daughter Betsey? She and her child had taken refuge in the fort with most of her fellow citizens who lived in the vicinity.

Something very odd was happening to Hull. He was becoming catatonic. His brain, overloaded by too much information, refused to function. His brigade major, Thomas Jesup, found his commander half-seated, half-crouched on an old tent lying on the ground. His back was to the ramparts under the curtain of the fort that faced the enemy. Except for the movement of his jaws he seemed comatose. He was chewing tobacco at a furious rate, filling his mouth with it, absently adding quid after quid, sometimes removing a piece, rolling it between his fingers and then replacing it, so that his hands ran with spittle, while the brown juice dribbled from the corners of his mouth, staining his neck cloth, his beard, his cravat, and his vest. He chewed as though the fate of the army depended upon the movement of his jaws, rubbing the lower half of his face from time to time until it, too, was stained dark brown.

Jesup had reconnoitred the British position. He asked Hull for permission to move up some artillery and attack their flank. Hull nodded but he was clearly out of control. All he could say, as much to himself as to Jesup, was that a cannon ball had killed four men.

It was the future as much as the present that rendered him numb. A procession of ghastly possibilities crowded his mind: his troops deserting pell mell to the enemy; the women and children starving through a long siege; cannon fire dismembering more innocent bystanders; finally – the ultimate horror – the Indians released by Brock and Tecumseh, bent on revenge for Tippecanoe and all that came before it, ravaging, raping, burning, killing.

He saw his daughter scalped, his grandchild mutilated, his friends and neighbours butchered. He believed himself outnumbered and outmanoeuvred, his plea for reinforcements unheeded. He was convinced that defeat was inevitable. If he postponed it the blood of innocent people would be on his hands. If he accepted it before the battle was joined he could save hundreds of lives. He could, of course, fight on to the last man and go down in the history books as a hero. But could he live with himself, however briefly, if he took the hero's course?

There was another thought too, a guilty thought, lurking like a vagrant in the darker recesses of that agitated mind.

The memory of the notorious proclamation returned to haunt him. He himself had threatened no quarter to any of the enemy who fought beside the Indians. Could he or his charges, then, expect mercy in a prolonged struggle? Might the enemy not use his own words to justify their allies' revenge?

The shells continued to scream and explode above his head. Six men were now dead, several more were wounded, the fort in a turmoil. Hull determined to ask for a cease-fire at a parley with Brock, scrawled a note to his son, Abraham – his aide-de-camp – and asked him to get it across the river. Incredibly it didn't occur to him that Brock might be already outside the palisades with his troops.

At the same time Hull ordered a white tablecloth hung out of a window where the British artillery commander on the Canadian shore could see it. He had no intention of fighting to the last. In the future metropolis of Detroit there would be no Hull Boulevard, no Avenue of Martyrs.

Abraham Hull tied a handkerchief to a pike and gave it to Major Josiah Snelling, Hull's aide. Snelling said he'd be damned if he'd disgrace his country by taking it out of the fort. Young Hull took it himself and crossed the river, only to discover that Brock was on the American side. When he got back, Snelling was persuaded to seek out the British general.

Outside the fort, Jesup, seeking to take command of the dragoons to meet Brock's expected attack, found the whole line breaking up and the men marching back toward the fort by platoons. Baffled, he asked what on earth was going on. An officer riding by told him: "Look to the fort!"

For the first time Jesup saw the white flag. He rode back, accosted Hull, and demanded to know if surrender was being considered. Hull's reply was unintelligible. Jesup urged Hull to hold out at least until McArthur and Cass returned, but all Hull could exclaim was, "My God, what shall I do with these women and children?"

Hull had already ordered the Ohio volunteers to retreat into the fort. Their commander, Colonel Findlay, rode up in a rage. "What the hell am I ordered here for?" he demanded. Hull replied in a trembling voice that several men had been killed and he believed he could obtain better terms from Brock if he capitulated now than if he were to wait for a storm or a siege.

"Terms!" shouted Findlay. "Damnation! We can beat them on the plain. I didn't come here to capitulate; I came here to fight!" He sought out Lieutenant-Colonel Miller, "The general talks of surrender, let us put him under arrest."

But Miller was a regular officer and no mutineer. "Colonel Findlay, I am a soldier. I shall obey my superior officer."

The shelling had ceased. Hidden in the ravine, Brock's men were enjoying breakfast provided by a British civilian who had refused to change allegiance when Detroit became an American community after the Revolution. The owner opened his doors to Brock's officers and the contents of pantry and cellar to his troops, who managed in this brief period to toss off twenty-four gallons (110 L) of brandy, fifteen gallons (68 L) of Madeira, and nine (41 L) of port.

In the midst of this unexpected revel, some of the men spotted Brock's two aides, Glegg and Macdonell, moving toward the fort with a flag of truce. Was it over so quickly?

Hull wanted a three day respite. Brock gave him three hours. After that he said he'd attack. After this no nonsense ultimatum it became clear that Hull was prepared for a full surrender. He would give up everything – the fort, its contents, all the ordnance, all supplies, all the troops, even those commanded by the absent colonels. *Everything*.

Hull tried to make some provision for those Canadian deserters who had come over to his side. Macdonell replied with a curt "totally inadmissible." Hull made no further objection and left the details of the surrender to his juniors.

Now, Brock rolled into the fort accompanied by a fife and drum corps. Fifteen-year-old John Richardson, chosen as a member of the advance guard, had never felt so proud than at this moment. But the guard had advanced a little too quickly. The articles of surrender stipulated the Americans must leave the fort before the British entered. A confused melee followed. The American soldiers were in turmoil, some crying openly, a few of the officers breaking their swords, and some of the soldiers breaking their muskets rather than surrender them. Others cried "treason!" and "treachery!" and heaped curses on their general's head. One of the Ohio volunteers tried to stab Macdonell before the advance guard moved back across the drawbridge.

Finally the tangle was straightened out. The Americans stacked their arms and moved out of the fort. The 4th Regiment of regulars, its members in despair and tears, gave up its colours sewn by a group of Boston ladies and carried through the battle of Tippecanoe.

Down came the Stars and Stripes. The Union Jack was hoisted high to the cheers of the troops. Young Richardson was one of those chosen to mount the first guard at the flagstaff. He strutted up and down at his post, peacock proud, casting his eyes down at the vanquished Americans on the esplanade below the fort.

Tecumseh knew many of the American prisoners and greeted them in Detroit without apparent rancour. Now in the aftermath of the bloodless victory more tales were added to his legend.

There was for instance, the story of Father Gabriel Richard, the priest of Ste. Anne's parish who refused to take the oath of allegiance to the Crown because he said he had already sworn an oath to support the American constitution. Procter imprisoned him at Sandwich and Tecumseh insisted on his release. Procter snubbed the Shawnee chief. Tecumseh swiftly assembled his followers and told Procter he would return to the Wabash River if the priest was not freed. The colonel gave in.

There are other tales. Tecumseh was speaking to his followers at the River Raisin when he felt a tug at his jacket and looked down and saw a small white girl. "Come to our house, there are bad Indians there," she said. He stopped his speech, seized his tomahawk, followed her, dropped the leader with one blow and, as the others moved to the attack, shouted out, "Dogs! I am Tecumseh!" When the Indians retreated Tecumseh entered the house and found British officers present. "You are worse than dogs to break faith with your prisoners!" he cried. The British apologized for not having restrained the Indians. They offered to place a guard on the house, but the child's mother told them it wasn't necessary. So long as Tecumseh was near she felt safe.

For the British, if not for the Indians, Detroit's surrender was staggering. Upper Canada, badly supplied and even worse armed, now had an additional cache of 2,500 captured muskets, thirty-nine heavy guns, forty barrels of gun powder, a sixteen-gun rig, a great many smaller craft, and a baggage train of one hundred pack animals and three hundred cattle, provisions and stores. The prize money to be distributed among the troops was reckoned at two hundred thousand dollars – an enormous sum considering that a private's net pay a month amounted to about four shillings – or one dollar a week. $1.⁰⁰/wk., net pay.
Every soldier received prize money of more than four pounds – at least twenty weeks net pay. The amount increased according to rank. Sergeants got eight pounds, captains forty pounds. Brock was due two hundred and sixteen pounds.

More significant was the fact that Brock had rolled back the entire frontier to the Ohio River, the line the Indians themselves claimed to be the border between white territories and their own lands. Most of Michigan Territory was now in British hands. Many Indians, such as the Mohawk of the Grand Valley, who had been reluctant to fight on either side, were now firmly and enthusiastically committed to the British cause. The same could be said for all the population of Upper Canada, once so lukewarm in defeat, now fired to enthusiasm by Brock's stunning victory. In Montreal, Quebec, the spectacle of Hull's tattered and ravaged followers invoked a wave of patriotic ardour.

In Canada, Isaac Brock was the man of the hour. In America, the very word "Hull" was used as a derogatory epithet. In their shame and despair, Americans of all political stripes lashed out blindly at the general who was universally considered to be a traitor and a coward.

But times and attitudes change. Today, one might ask, who was the real hero? Was it Isaac Brock, who was quite prepared, if forced, to let his Indian allies run wild through the fort, slaying men, women and children. (Could Tecumseh have prevented a blood bath?) Or was it Hull, the compassionate old soldier, who decided to surrender rather than see his people needlessly destroyed?

Hull was made the scapegoat for all of Washington's bumbling. When he was finally exchanged he faced a court martial that was a travesty of a trial. His lawyer was not permitted to cross examine those officers who came up against him or to examine other witnesses. The old general, untrained in the law, had to perform that task himself. Nor was he allowed to examine copies of his personal papers.

The court was packed against him and he was eventually found guilty of cowardice.

Hull was sentenced to be shot, but the President took into account his revolutionary gallantry, and pardoned him. He spent the rest of his life attempting to vindicate his actions. It's an irony of war that had he refused to surrender, had he gone down to defeat, his fort and town shattered by cannon fire, his friends and neighbours ravaged by the misfortunes of battle, his soldiers dead to the last man, the civilians burned out, bombed out, and inevitably scalped, the tired old general would have been swept into the history books as a gallant martyr, his name enshrined on bridges, schools, main streets, and public buildings.

But for the rest of their lives, the very soldiers who, because of him, could now go back whole to the comfort of their homesteads, and the civilians, who were now able to pick up the strings of their existence, only briefly tangled, would loathe and curse the name of William Hull who, on his deathbed at the age of seventy-two, would continue to insist that he took the only proper, decent, and courageous course on that bright August Sunday in 1812.

Index

Don't Miss

THE DEATH OF ISAAC BROCK

Pierre Berton continues the story of the
War of 1812
with his graphic description of the most significant battle
in Canadian history: The British-Canadian victory at
Queenston Heights.

How a small force of regular soldiers, volunteers and
Mohawk Indians trapped and defeated a much larger
American army and saved Upper Canada from becoming
part of the United States.

And how the nation's greatest general, dashing up the
heights above the Niagara River, died bravely but
incautiously, thus creating an imperishable legend.